W9-BWP-778

THE UNIVERSITY OF MAINE
AT AUGUSTA
WITHDRAWN
from
Katz Library, U.M.A.
BENNETT D. KATZ LIBRARY

OPERATION HAZALAH

OPERATION HAZALAH

by Gilles Lambert

Translated by Robert Bullen and Rosette Letellier

THE BOBBS-MERRILL COMPANY, INC.
INDIANAPOLIS / NEW YORK

Published by the Bobbs-Merrill Company, Inc.
Indianapolis/New York

ISBN 0-672-51878-6
Library of Congress catalog card number 73-11791
Designed by Paula Wiener
Manufactured in the United States of America

First printing

Acknowledgments

This story could not have been completed without the active collaboration of Auguste Dordan. Having lived through the tragic events in Hungary in 1944, he was able to provide careful cross-checking to support various statements. His knowledge of Hungarian, German, and Hebrew was invaluable throughout the course of this inquiry.

I also wish to express my sincere gratitude to the following: the Yad Washem Institute (Martyrs and Heroes Memorial Authority), Jerusalem; the Centre de Documentation Juive Contemporaine, Paris; and the Kibbutz of the Ghetto Combatants.

I also wish to thank the following individuals: Efra Agmon, Tel Aviv; David Assael, Ramat-Chen, Israel; Pnina Blum, Tel Aviv; Judge Cholon Breslauer, Israel; Dan Billitzer, Jerusalem; Nicolas Birnbaum, Paris; Tibor Dery, Tel Aviv; Emmeric Deutsch, Paris; Elisabeth Eppler, London; Pauli, Paris; Jenö Frankl, Jerusalem; Mr. Friedman, Neve Mihaël, Israel; Andreas Gal, New York; Sandor Gervai, Jerusalem; Zvi Goldfarb, Jerusalem; Coça Grunwalt, Jerusalem; Grand Rabbi Fabian

Herschkovitz, Tel Aviv; Mr. G. Haymon, Tel Aviv; Mr. G. Katona, New York; Josy Katz, Ramat Gan, Israel; David Klein, Tel Aviv; Moshe Krausz, Jerusalem; Professor Löwinger, Jerusalem; Consul Charles Lutz, Berne; Mme. Magen, Jerusalem; Mr. Noetchke, Jerusalem; Pinchas Rosenbaum, Geneva; Michel Salomon, Tel Aviv; Rabbi Schreiber-Sofer, Jerusalem; Abraham Schweizer, Tel Aviv; Samuel Springmann, Tel Aviv; Professor Tennen, Jerusalem; Vilmas Weiss, New York; Moshe Weiskopf, Jerusalem; Professor Yaron, Jerusalem; Major Stephane Yrmi, Jerusalem; Simon Zussman, Jerusalem.

Contents

Where there is no man, do your best to be a man.
Rabbi Hillel (70 B.C.)

Where is God?
—"He is there, hanged."
Elie Wiesel

Here and there young people take up arms or escape. Here and there underground shelters, fortified bunkers, defense lines are built. Here and there people prepare for an insurrection that would teach mankind and history a lesson they hardly deserve.
Elie Wiesel

OPERATION HAZALAH

Introduction

LATE NOVEMBER 1944. In the middle of the night, under an icy rain, two SS officers walk through Budapest. The city seems paralyzed, in agony. It belongs to the Nylas, the Hungarian Nazis, brought to power by the occupying Germans. Without trial and with refinements of cruelty they kill those Jews who fall into their hands. Every night hundreds of Jewish men, women, and children are tortured, shot on the banks of the Danube, or thrown alive into the river. At dawn one sees red stains on the drifting ice. And every morning the hunt resumes.

The two SS, in long leather coats, their caps stamped with the death's head, have that slow and domineering gait that characterizes the elite Nazi corps. They near the hospital on Wesselenyi Street—their hospital. Suddenly, from behind a building looms another patrol—two other SS coming in their direction.

Two shots in the night—which awaken nobody. Two of the SS collapse: the two coming from the hospital. The real ones. The others stride over the bodies and continue on their way. The two are Jews; one is a theology student, the son of a rabbi from the northern part of the country who was gassed in Auschwitz with the rest of his family several months ago. The other is an agricultural student. Both are Zionists, pioneers. By an amazing coincidence, the Nazi hospital they are about to enter—in an attempt to free one of their comrades—is situated a short distance from the birthplace of Theodore Herzl, the founder of Zionism. Their mission is extraordinarily risky—almost hopeless.

In Budapest, during the latter part of 1944, under death's dictatorship, reason has lost its rights. And the rebellious young Hungarian Zionists, stirred up in response to the massacre, have foresworn any calculation of risk. Hatred without motive, death without reason envelop them. They respond to absurdity with acts of absurd daring. Almost without weapons, without support (there is no Resistance in Hungary), they cannot reasonably succeed. In a world where madness prevails, their last chance is to defy reason.

Absurdity is surely what characterizes the extermination of the Hungarian Jews—the ultimate stage of the "final solution." When it begins, more than five million European Jews have already perished. The Axis defeat is taken for granted. The landing in the West is imminent, and the Red Army advances irresistibly. Hungary seeks every means of getting out of the war.

By all logic, one can assume that the Nazis will throw their ultimate resources into a last-ditch resistance or survival operation; that they will bridle their exterminating fury. The opposite occurs; experience accumulated in other occupied countries of Europe enables the defeated Nazis to perform a final superefficient, exemplary operation. Between May and July 1944, 500,000 Hungarian Jews are shipped to the gas chambers—the output of which has been improved. The last trains leaving Hungary transport Jewish families from Budapest, their destination the crematory ovens. And when the railroads become unusable, the Nazis drive their victims on foot, over the roads, under the fire from Soviet cannons.

Eichmann was to derive great pride from this model operation; speed and efficiency records were broken. Records for cruelty too, because of the help lent by the Hungarian Nazis to the expedited plan of deportation, and because of the assent of nearly the whole of the population.

The liquidation of Hungarian Jews was, for the Nazis, the most successful action of the final solution. Historically it was marked by several other particulars. The world's conscience awoke, alerted, no doubt, by approaching victory. Great voices spoke out in behalf of the Hungarian Jews. Neutral diplomats, even in Budapest, began to act with courage. The rapid development of the military situation also favored the opening of negotiations with the Nazis; Himmler launched his famous proposal—1,000,000 condemned Jews for 10,000 trucks.

Finally, the last of the great Nazi exercises in collective murder gave birth to one of the most desperate, most dramatic, least-known resistance movements in the history of World War II.

This movement was essentially the work of Hungarian Zionists, young partisans known as the *halutzim*. Boys and girls, religious or not, of every political stripe, they stood up to the exterminator. Raised in the spirit of the *Aliyah*,* hardened, they defied the Nazi law, the yellow star, the herding,

* *Aliyah,* meaning the "going up" to Israel, was the name of the Zionist organization that helped Jews all over the world to emigrate to Palestine.

the ghetto, the deportation. Doubly isolated in a hostile country and within a community that to the end believed (or wanted to believe) in negotiation, they launched forth, almost without means, practically without weapons, into an unequal, almost hopeless confrontation. In a city that was the prey of criminal madness, theirs was a rescuing madness. One saw skinny adolescents put on SS uniforms, penetrate to the heart of enemy bastions, and accomplish incredible missions. One saw students from the *yeshivas* (Talmudic schools) and from other religious schools, disguised as stooges of the "Arrow Cross"—the Hungarian Nazis—force prison doors; boy and girl messengers carrying false IDs pass through a hundred nets set up by the police, the gendarmerie, the army; children without weapons attack groups of armed, trained men.

It was Operation Hazalah. In Hebrew, Hazalah means "rescue." Most of those who took part in the operation lost their lives in it—dying of torture, shot down in the streets, thrown into the Danube. Their families, their community were wiped out; even the memory of them vanished. Those who survived, settled today in Israel or elsewhere in the world, do not look upon themselves as heroes. Their action saved part of Hungarian Judaism; 100,000 Jews, perhaps more, owe them their lives. But human lives are not numbers to be added up. As we read in the Talmud: "Whoever contributes to the salvation of a single man is as worthy as if he had saved all mankind."

ONE

The Last European Jews in Peril

SUNDAY MARCH 19, 1944. At the beginning of the day, the advance party of the German army, made up of a few motorcycles and cars, enters Budapest by Margaret Bridge, preceding the tanks. Since dawn the royal palace, the airports, and strategic points in the city have been occupied by paratroopers. Hungary, the Axis ally, becomes an occupied country.

It is no surprise to the inhabitants of Budapest. For weeks they have been expecting an "occupation" of the country. At eight o'clock the radio broadcasts a laconic communiqué: "By the terms of an agreement concluded between the new government and the Reich chancellory, the German troops will be temporarily stationed in Hungary. The duty of the population is to provide a warm welcome to our faithful companions in arms."

On their way to cafés and pastry shops, on this beautiful, cold, and luminous day, people exchange all kinds of "news." It is said that Regent Horthy, who three days ago was brutally summoned to Hitler's headquarters, is being held prisoner (this is false: when he arrived at the palace, at ten in the morning, he was greeted by a guard of German soldiers). It is said that Prime Minister Kallay has taken refuge at the Turkish embassy (this will be confirmed). It is said, a little prematurely, that the Allied armies are on the eve of landing in the West. It is whispered, and will soon be confirmed, that the police, infiltrated by pro-Nazis, have just thrown Socialist politicians into jail, as well as liberal journalists, opponents of Axis politics, and eminent Jews.

In this swirl of news, rumors, predictions, and interpretations, one certainty is common to Hungarians of all persuasions, all origins, all religions: the unsettled fate of their country has taken a new turn.

Many of them still hope that Hungary, faithful ally of the Axis, will succeed in getting out of the conflict without too much harm. It is six months since Italy changed camps; the Red Army irresistibly nears the Carpathians; the Anglo-Americans are ready for the final assault. No doubt the Regent has engaged in negotiations with the Allies. But the hope of a separate peace fades forever that Sunday morning, with the thundering of the German tanks. Hungary is plunged into war and into defeat—more deeply, more desperately than ever.

Along the avenues and boulevards, where the pale sun melts the last patches of snow, Sunday crowds stroll; the churches are full; there are lines in front of the Turkish-bath establishments and at the Opéra box office. Groups form at the doors of the pastry shops; in the inns of Buda, tired Tziganes clean up the traces of boisterous nightlife. Laughter is heard—but anxiety prevails. In the afternoon, at the football stadium, the game between the championship teams of Budapest and Ferencvaros attracts few people: the Hungarians are gathered around their radio sets. Anxiety is keener among the Jews.

At this time there are more than 900,000 of them in Hungary: the national community has almost doubled following the annexation to Hungary of a part of Transylvania, a part of Slovakia and other territories—and with the arrival of Slovakian and Polish refugees. Paradoxically—for Hungary was the first country in Europe to be under anti-Semitic jurisdiction—the Jews enjoy a certain security; none of them has been deported to a concentration camp. The only missing Jews were the victims of a raid organized by the gendarmerie in 1941 (the non-Hungarian Jews arrested were driven back into territory occupied by the Germans, and almost all of them assassinated), or were among those recruited for forced labor and sent behind the Hungarian and German lines in the U.S.S.R. Nearly 50,000 Jews have perished, most of them at the hands of Hungarian soldiers.

Hungary is a shelter—fragile, precarious—but a shelter nonetheless; other countries occupied by the Nazis in Europe were *Judenrein:* purified of their Jews, or on the verge of being so, in varying degrees. Enlarged by influxes from abroad, the Hungarian community is the only one almost intact in occupied Europe.

It is alive, manifold, a true microcosm of the Diaspora; every category of European Jew is represented here. In Hungary everything is extreme: The assimilated, wealthy bourgeois patriots are perhaps more assimilated, more nationalistic than anywhere else. The religious Orthodox, living in respect for the traditions, are more religious, more orthodox than anywhere else. Their synagogues, their *yeshivas,* their rabbis and their *tsaddiks*—their "Just"—seem to belong to another age. The Zionists, the great majority of them young, whether religious or not, Communist or moderate, are ardent partisans —wasn't Theodore Herzl, founder of the movement, born in Budapest?

They are truly, though Hungary may not be aware of it, the "rear guard" of European Judaism. Faced with the danger that has become more acute with the arrival of soldiers from the Third Reich and with the inevitable coming to power of the ferocious anti-Semite Sztojai; faced with the now more precise and direct threats of extermination, this group ought to unite, to become one. It will, however, be divided. Ideological conflicts, divergences, oppositions will develop; unbridgeable gaps will open between fathers and sons, young and old, community and community. Responding to the wishes of the Nazi exterminators, who have learned in other occupied countries of Europe how to turn their future victims against themselves in order to better dominate them, the Hungarian Jews, during that dramatic spring of 1944, are deeply divided in their evaluations of the risks, on what attitude to adopt in the face of the danger, and on the proper means for facing it.

The ambiguities of the situation, the multiplicity of political and religious doctrine and opinion, the lack of information and the flow of false rumors, the intoxication—in short, the near-impossibility of "judging"—explain these divisions. The enemy had many faces. The holocaust—the massive extermination—became a reality only after the war. Before that, it was inconceivable, even for the Jews. Most of all for them. These tragic divisions among Hungarian Jews reflect a crisis growing out of an inability to understand.

The victory of the Allies seemed imminent. Encircled, pushed back, beaten on all fronts, were not the Nazis on the eve of capitulation? With all their might, with an unreasonable fervor, the vast majority of Hungarian Jews try to believe that they will be saved by the course of events. Why would the enemy, amid the disaster, prolong the massacre of innocents—all information about this massacre being in any case contradictory? Even if the Nazis wanted to put the last touch to their work of death, they would lack the time and the means to do it. Hadn't two years been needed to deport 50,000 Jews from Slovakia? "Time," think most of the Hungarian Jews, "works for us."

And the Nazis will feed this illusion. Nowhere outside Hungary have the SS made so many "contacts," started so many "negotiations," opened so many doors, the sooner to close them on hopes for liberation, rescue, exchange or the "buying back" of hostages. Today it is known that Himmler was anxious to secure personal guarantees for the postwar period. Through various intermediaries, he had for a year been in contact with representatives of international Judaism. The intact Hungarian community was his ultimate currency. In Hungary, in a context of anguish and obscurity, the "overtures" were interpreted by the Jews to be proofs of weakness founded on the certainty of defeat. In them they read the promise that the community would be spared—with a little luck. And that is exactly how the SS wanted them to be understood. The insane hope these overtures engendered among the Hungarian Jews would lessen, they thought, the potential for resistance, for never had the Nazis seriously considered sparing the last Jews of Europe. The Nuremberg trials dispelled all doubt on the subject. "Maybe we were going to be defeated," declared Schmidt, Hungary's executioner, "but at least we would have accomplished that task." And Eichmann expressed satisfaction at the "rapidity" of the action against the Hungarian Jews.

The illusion of a respite reached the free world, attentive but curiously paralyzed and mute in the face of the immense genocide that continued to be carried out. In his book *While Six Million Died,* Arthur Morse writes: "The Germans' quickness to act in Hungary caught the world by surprise, for at that time the defeat of the Axis was certain and a softening of anti-Semitic persecutions was expected." Contrary to what they thought, time was not on the side of the Jews, abandoned as they were by everyone. In the face of the hurried exterminators, they could count only on themselves. And on God.

In Him, the pious Jews of provincial communities, the guardians of the Faith, the *Hasidim*, with their inspired and peaceful faces, the Orthodox, careful to observe the least precepts of the Law, placed their unshakable hope. They delivered themselves up to His justice, indifferent to the turns and vagaries of politics, to the changes in government; deaf to threats. Accustomed to persecutions and pogroms, survivors of massacres for centuries, familiars of hatred, they refused to admit that the very nature of hatred had changed. Their prayers, their meditations, their observance of ritual kept them on the margin of an undecipherable world. While the assimilated Jews watched for the favorable acceleration of events, the Orthodox found shelter in that slowing of time that prayer provides and which is the essence of God. The former counted on the passing days, the latter counted on eternity—conflicting illusions which death by gas would tragically reconcile in several months. There exists a photographic document taken by a Nazi souvenir collector, representing a group of Hungarian rabbis debarking from the death train on a platform at Auschwitz. One knows what the trip had been like: from out of the night these men discover turmoil, the howlings of the Nazis, the welcoming commandos of kapos, the whips, the dogs. Hell. In a few moments they will be gassed. They gather and look at the photographer. In their eyes there is nothing but indifference and contempt. They are detached, absent. For them reality has already lost meaning. These pious Jews have accepted death. A world where such acts take place is not the world of God. It is not theirs.

How many were there in Hungary, religious or not, who rejected illusion, the refuge of hope, and accepted reality—having decided to face it? A few thousand—at that point. Most of them young. And Zionist.

The existence of death camps is for them a familiar reality. The notion of extermination is not beyond them. They know through the stories of escapees what Treblinka and Maidanek were—before their destruction by the Nazis—what Auschwitz is, how the death industry works, and at what tempo. Refugees from Poland or Slovakia have told them of their hallucinatory experiences. They know everything about the death trains, the selection on the arrival platform, the gas chambers, the crematories, the recovery of hair, gold teeth, human fat. They know that the fate of those who escape immediate death is even worse: forced labor, human experimentation, and, worst of all, the auxiliary exterminating commandos. They also know in detail the tragedy of the Warsaw uprising during Easter of the previous year. On both sides, death. On one side, a passive death. On the other, a man's death—a Zionist's, a combatant's. They have made their choice.

But how to make their choice understood by the divided community, which is scared, confident, and thoroughly "manipulated" by a diabolic and experienced enemy? The young don't believe that "corrupted" Nazis exist or that there are Nazis willing to deal with Jews. They are right, as history will prove. Unhappily, at this moment they feel only mistrust and hostility from the Jews.

Aid from the outside also seems improbable. These Zionists have practically no contacts with the free world, with the Allies. A few emissaries have succeeded in reaching Palestine, by way of Turkey, but little is expected from their missions. As it is, to support the Jewish resistance taking shape in Hungary, the Palestinian partisans will be able to put into action only three inexperienced paratrooper commandos. These three—Hanna Szenes, Joel Palgi, and Perez Goldstein—will be betrayed, arrested as soon as they enter Hungary, and neutralized. Hanna Szenes, shot soon afterward in Budapest, is to become a great heroine to all Jewish combatants.

Nothing more. The Zionists have no help, no friends, no arms. No national resistance, as in France or in Poland, to give them a hand. No partisans. No parachute drops to hope for. Not even radio liaison with London, or comforting and mysterious "personal messages." The country—their country? —is on the whole favorable to measures that strike at the Jews, insistently pointed to as responsible for the war, for the misfortunes of the times. This hostility, which events will reinforce, is soon to give their action its almost desperate character.

Within the Jewish community, the resistance they plan appears to be a serious threat to the policy of waiting, negotiating, haggling. The Jews of Budapest have no sympathy for these youths, Zionist and even sometimes Communist, who are organizing for an armed fight. Deep inside, the well-provided "assimilated" Jews, the Budapest bourgeois, believe that they are all, individually, safe from deportation. They calculate that in paying, in discussing, in making the most of the resources of Jewish dialectic, in gaining time, they will save their skins. Not all of them, perhaps—war is war—but the majority will survive. And each of them sees himself and those closest to him in this majority. In March 1944 Dr. Rezsö Kastner, a courageous Zionist but a negotiator by temperament (as the organizer of the famous Bergen-Belsen convoy, he was tried in Israel after the war, declared not guilty, and later assassinated), wrote about the young Zionists of Budapest preparing for combat: "The Zionist core, the youth, *with their upsetting preparations for resistance*, will remain isolated among the Jews."

Pious Jews, especially in the provinces, also prove to be hostile to this arming for action. To them—pacifistic, gentle, introspective, myopic—any idea of material resistance is alien. A Jew does not carry arms. For them, to fight is to fall from the spiritual summit to the bestial level of the adversary, to abandon the privileges of meditation, of faith, of submission to divine will. It is tantamount to repudiating the Judaic faith. "Maybe we will die," they think, "but as martyrs; never as executioners . . ."

Thwarted by some, misunderstood by others, the young Zionists of Budapest have nothing in their favor but their ideal, and the certainty of their choice. Many had been ready to go to Israel; just before the war they had endured the harsh training of pioneers, the *halutzim*, on community farms in Hungary. Their bodies are hardened; their souls are prepared for the fight. Not to be able to share this determination with other Jews who are deaf to their arguments, insensitive to their demonstrations, is for them an additional ordeal. They know they are sacrificed. And alone in their sacrifice.

Yet their reasoning is irrefutable. We know today that wherever the Jews were submissive, wherever they obeyed the laws and decrees, they were exterminated; while wherever the spirit of resistance prevailed, the Nazis had to abandon part of their spoils. Whenever the Jews escaped, refused to gather in ghettos, became partisans, and defied their enemies, the rate of losses decreased spectacularly. In his book *The Revolt of the Just*, historian Lucien Steinberg compares the case of Kiev—where there was only one survivor out of more than 33,000 Jews—with that of White Russia—where more than half the population survived. In the latter, Jewish partisans spontaneously sprang up in the marshes.

Budapest's young Zionists were right in preparing for resistance and combat, even though, in those first bright days of the spring of 1944, it seemed suicidal.

TWO

The Zionists' Defiance

FOR MONTHS, young religious Zionists of Budapest's Misrahi have been meeting every day in their local on Laudon Street, the street of leather tanners, in the heart of the Jewish quarter. The neighbors, poor and peaceable artisans, thought that these boys and girls, some of them barely fourteen years old, were preparing a theatrical production, or getting set for the traditional Lag B'omer excursion—the big springtime country picnic in honor of the Jewish heroes Bar Khokba and Rabbi Akiba. Hadn't these Misrahi youths given their movement the name of Ben Akiba—son of the combatant-rabbi killed in the desperate rebellion against the Romans—the Son of the Star?

Only a few initiates knew it was not a matter of a celebration or a picnic, and the spirit prevailing among these young religious Zionists was one of revolt, of ardent fight and sacrifice, like that at the time of the great uprising against the Romans.

Their faces betrayed nothing; they joked, they laughed on their way to movement headquarters. Their gaiety was not meant simply to fool the Hungarians, or the Nazi spies who arrogantly, provokingly, circulated through the poor streets of Budapest's Jewish quarter; it was genuine, the kind of gaiety inherent in youth, which nothing can alter—not even approaching tragedy or the shadow of death. None of them, however, cultivated illusions; the refugees from Poland, from Slovakia, the escapees from the death camps whom the movement had sheltered and hidden had brought sufficient testimony to lift whatever doubts remained: it was decisively a war of extermination that the Nazis had declared on the Jews of Europe. An absurd war—but one without mercy.

For a long time the youthful Zionists had been organizing escape networks in collaboration with other Budapest Zionist organizations. In turn they went to the borders under assumed names in order to maintain the few connections that allowed entry into Rumania, at the same time keeping the doors of Hungary open to a few Slovakian Jews. They gave money to "escape agents" who often denounced them. They tried to set up contacts. The escape networks to Rumania were offered to refugees too shaken by their experience to be able to play a role in the Resistance; many escapees, in fact, were on the edge of madness. They had seen their families perish amidst atrocious suffering. They had themselves traveled through hell. Their nerves shattered, their minds devastated, haunted by the scenes they had witnessed, they thought only of fleeing Europe.

The young partisans of B'ni Akiba called one of these hazardous trips a *tijoul*—"excursion" in Hebrew. Very few of the candidates for the Promised Land got as far as the Rumanian coast. And even once on board a scow their adventure was not over. But the escape agents were kept in business. Those who betrayed—cashing their pay from both the Jews and the Nazis—were replaced. The risk was inevitable—and one had to accept it.

Other partisans were in charge of filling the supply of false "Aryan" papers and false IDs, for the moment was near when Jews, if they were to escape their destiny, would have to abandon their identities.

In Hungary, in fact, "religion" was part of one's civil status and appeared on official documents. A census, with the stamping of papers, would not even be necessary: lists of Jews were ready.

The partisans also applied themselves to copying or duplicating texts and testimonies from the refugees, in the hope of shaking the apathy and the refusal to understand of the other Jews in Budapest. But the task was difficult. The heated discussions always ended in the same way:

"You are too young—and you are Zionists," answered the elders. "Your 'advanced' ideas mask reality for you. Hungary is not like the other countries. What happened in Poland or Slovakia cannot happen here."

The Zionists could do nothing but pool their disappointments and copy for distribution around town the latest testimonies of death-camp escapees. Against them stood not only the Nazi enemy—implacable, lucid, and organized—but also the Jews of Hungary—hesitant, weak, and blind.

It was singularly harrowing, but they had the vague feeling that they were placed by fate at a turning point in the history of Judaism. How to penetrate and bend the mentality of those "assimilated," confident Hungarian Jews? Hungary was indeed a special case in Europe. Anti-Semitism, an element of daily life there, no doubt had deeper foundations than anywhere else in Europe. And this certainly made the young Zionists' enterprise no easier.

It was Hungary which, as early as 1924, had promulgated the first discriminatory laws against Jews. Semifeudal, the

Magyars had no need of fascism to discover in the Jew the hereditary enemy. And yet the situation in no way impeded "assimilation." If Judaism was suspect and despised, Jews were accepted, integrated, and sometimes even honored by the whole nation; there were Jews at the highest levels of the government. The grand rabbi of Budapest was by rights a member of the high legislative chamber. The most popular actor in the country, Rosahegyi, was of Jewish origin; ironically, he specialized in Magyar peasant roles, crude and anti-Semitic almost by definition. It was a strange picture—but falsely reassuring. The partisans sensed it; the danger might be hidden, but that did not lessen the peril. But their voices did not carry. They were young, suspect. And, as Zionists, dangerous.

They worked at arming themselves, organizing themselves militarily, establishing caches for arms and "bunkers" for men. In the absence of modern weapons, knives and axes were stored. The youths who had received an embryonic military training on the farms passed it on to the others. Their souls were steeled to the approach of the test, their ardent faith in God founded on a mighty will for the fight. The "Sons of the Star" gathered their energy. In their refusal to submit, they drew upon an ardent spiritual exaltation.

Among the Misrahi partisans are two Polish youths, survivors of Warsaw. They were hidden in the Christian part of the city under false identities. They survived the desperate explosion, the agony of the ghetto. Refugees in Hungary, they have come upon a familiar situation. The Nazi enemy is ready for action. They "know," with even more certainty than the others, that negotiation is an illusion. For them, there is only one response: uprising. But sooner—and stronger—than in Warsaw.

And yet even the young Hungarians argue with them:

"In Warsaw, those in the ghetto were not alone. We know

it. In '43 some of our boys got into the Warsaw ghetto—and returned to Budapest. The Jews of the ghetto's secret Zionist army benefited from the aid—limited but real—of the partisans. They had contacts, messengers who got into the Christian part of the city by way of the sewers and the streetcars. They received arms and ammunition. Here we have almost nothing. It would be bare-fisted, derisive combat."

There is no Resistance in Hungary, no partisans. The Resistance is an opposition force—a reflex, a refusal. It is a reaction to a rape. Yet Hungary has not been raped by the Nazis; she has given herself, abandoned herself. No partisans, no underground networks, no radio liaison with the free world. Discussion always comes out at the same dead end.

A resistance network, a Pole confirms, lives only by the contribution from outside and by the support of a part of the population. It must be not only "protected" but supplied, and must have its own intelligence agents all the way to the enemy. The Jewish army of the Warsaw ghetto could never have been formed, with its meager arsenal, without a Christian Resistance on the outside.

Then what? The treads of the Nazi tanks make the streets of Budapest quake far into the night. London radio, which is very hard to receive because of the jamming, announces the entry of the Nazi troops into Hungary and interprets the operation as an act of panic on the part of Hitler. Victory is near, asserts the London announcer. But the young Jews of Budapest refuse the easy, tempting, blinding optimism.

"I remember the sadness, almost the despair you could read on certain faces in early March of '44," recounts one of the survivors. "Such a desire for action, and so few means! The refugees, the escapees who had united with us, shook with anger. They were haunted by memories of nighttime arrests, which we were yet to know, by the convoys, the sealed railroad cars, the death camps. We knew; *they* had seen! One of them, who had succeeded in reaching Budapest almost by miracle, holing up by day, walking by night, harbored by peasants or sometimes by priests, remained silent most of the time. But whenever he felt that the will of the others was wavering in the face of the difficulties, he began to tell in a muffled voice what he had seen with his own eyes at Treblinka: Jews digging a huge trench—their own grave—and lining up on the edge with Tommy guns trained on them; little Jewish children in a nearby forest, hurled into the air by the legs, serving as targets for pistol-shooting contests. He told it all in the same tone. Pregnant women disemboweled by bayonets, Polish rabbis on their knees waiting for the shot of the revolver in the back of the head, condemned children dancing and laughing in an attempt to stir pity in the SS. His brother, his father, his mother killed before his eyes.

" 'Expect no grace from them,' he used to say. 'If they can, they will kill every Hungarian Jew, to the last one . . .'

"We remained mute, crushed by the horror, mad with a desire for revenge. Sometimes, someone said, 'The end of the war is almost here.' But there was always a refugee to wave aside this shadow of a doubt if not of hope: 'Don't believe it, they'll find time to kill us all! Deportations and massacre have taught the rare survivors, but they have also taught the Nazis. They know how to divide our communities and sow discord among us, the better to wipe them out. They have perfected their techniques; transportation to the death camps is speeded up; the death factories are far better equipped—their output increases every day.' "

And dawn surprised the partisans, unable as they were to get any sleep, trembling with the desire to convince their fellow Jews, to declare their defiance by taking action and still survive.

On Laudon Street, the most awaited event was the arrival of a messenger—from the border, from the provinces, or even from the residential areas of Budapest. What were people thinking, what was going on out there? Often the messenger was a girl, chosen for her "Christian" look. Sometimes she would collapse in tears as soon as she arrived: she had escaped a road block or a raid, but her boy or girl companion (most of the time the messenger was doubled for security reasons) had been arrested.

On Sunday, the 19th, messengers and news arrive by the minute. From the fragmentary information, the Zionists seek to extract some idea of what's happening. It appears that the Nazis are already active in the city. They penetrated the grand consistory (Sip Street) and the Orthodox consistory (Dob Street). At the grand consistory they entered empty offices. The watchman received the order to summon all the officials for the next day, the 20th; "Baron Wisliceny," the SS commanding officer, has an urgent communication to deliver to them. (This sounds like bad news to the partisans; they rightly see in it the announcement of the creation of a *Judenrat*—a Jewish council—recalling the one that operated in Warsaw until the suicide of its president.)

At the Orthodox consistory—which also shelters the synagogue, schools, and residences—the SS gathered everyone in the courtyard. The head of the school, the *shammes* (the Sexton), men, women, and children were lined up along a wall, hands up, under the threat of Tommy guns. Laughing, the Nazis told them they were going to shoot them. "And the Jewish vermin of this whole country will get it too," one of them added.

Calmly the Jews began to recite the *Schma Israel,* the prayer of death, while the Nazis, laughing, rampaged through the offices. The agonizing scene dragged on for more than two hours. Then the jeering SS told the Jews to go: "Scatter among the other Jews; we'll know how to find you!"

As the poor victims headed for the street, the SS fired into the air, hastening their flight. They left guards on the grounds as well as in the grand consistory.

The account of these events in itself is fraught with menace; it can only strengthen the Zionists in their determination. But what will be its effect on the other Jews of Buda? In the end, the Nazis released two prisoners.

And what will be the message of this SS "baron"? One can imagine everything and fear everything, most of all because of the reassuring rumors—propagated by whom?—that begin to spread in the city. One is that the Pope has just made a solemn protest and that Roosevelt is going to direct a message to the Nazis, enjoining them to put an end to their homicidal fury.

The Zionists sense what these false appeasements and veiled hopes conceal. It is entirely in the Nazis' interest to foster the illusion of security among the Jews they are about to massacre. As an enraged refugee expressed it:

"To admit that the Nazis are about to stop the extermination of our people, even under external pressure, is to make a fatal error. It is to fall into *their* trap! They will kill Jews up to the last moment—up to their last ounce of strength."

Discussions of this sort, leading to the same conclusions, occur in the other Zionist movements—among the Hachomer Hazair and the Hanoar Hazioni, for example. Combating the false hopes raised by the Nazis is the most urgent task. That, and preparing for action—an action that must be mutual; as far as possible, decisions will be coordinated.

On Sunday night those responsible hold a meeting; a joint command of the Zionist resistance of Budapest is created almost spontaneously. Its chiefs will change quite often; because of other assignments, missions, arrests, the contact will often be cut off, but the adoption of common objectives is already the start of a strategy.

At dawn on Monday the first men of the Sonderheinsatzkommando of Standartenführer Eichmann settle themselves in the Majestic Hotel, requisitioned by the Nazis, on the hill called Svabhegy (Schwabenberg) in Buda.

THREE

The Nazi Plan

IN THE following days Eichmann arrives in Budapest accompanied by the most illustrious representatives of the famous IV A Service of the Gestapo. They include Dannecker, who directed the deportation in Bulgaria, France, and Italy; Wisliceny and Brunner, exterminators of Slovakia and Greece; Abromeit, just arrived from Yugoslavia; Siegfried Seidl and Burger from Theresienstadt; and Herman Krumey, Lodz executioner from Vienna. From Berlin, Eichmann has summoned his friends Rolf Günther and Franz Novak, and his "legal expert," Otto Munsche. These men, decorated, smiling, and serene, are already responsible for the silent massacre of more than 5,000,000 Jews in the "mills" (as they refer to them) of Auschwitz, Treblinka, Maidanek, and elsewhere. In recent days they have been together rarely, each having been detached to separate "actions." The Hungarian problem must be special. In fact it is: time presses; the fortunes of war are going against the Nazis; the Hungarian community is populous and wealthy—and Himmler, at least officially, grows impatient. They must strike quickly and hard. Such is the "historical" mission that the Sondereinsatzkommando men prepare themselves for.

Of course the transcripts of these meetings have never been found. But notes, reports, and interrogations have permitted reconstructions of them. No doubt they began with a statistical analysis of the situation, followed by a study of the state of mind prevailing in the Jewish community of Hungary—on its divisions. Here rested the real strength of the SS—not in numbers, since the leading crew at the Majestic never numbered more than thirty or so agents. Among the first decisions agreed upon were to put an intelligence system in operation and, naturally, to create a *Judenrat,* a Jewish council.

Up to that time, "counterespionage" in Budapest was taken care of by agents of the famous Admiral Canaris, under the embassy, and by Schellenberg's people. But now, in accord with Dr. Edmund Veesenmayer, who is to become the real Nazi *Gauleiter* of Hungary, Eichmann succeeds in having this activity entrusted from then on to the SS men of Sturmbannführer von Clages. Eichmann is not unaware that Canaris's services have established relations with Hungarian Jewish organizations and have even, on occasion, freed some condemned people, in exchange for postwar guarantees or even for sums of money. Himmler is not opposed to these contacts, but he insists that the negotiations—which will develop—be now controlled by his operatives. No doubt he is thinking of his own future. In any case, Colonel von Clages is assigned the mission of keeping secret the "action" under preparation—he is also to nip in the bud any organized opposition on the part of the Jews. The memory of the armed uprising of the Warsaw ghetto haunts the SS. Victims of their own propaganda, they were almost stupefied at the violence of this heroic resistance. Goebbels's diary, for the date of May 1, 1943, discloses an almost naïve echo of this astonishment: "You can see what the Jews are capable of when they are armed!"

As a priority, Himmler has ordered Eichmann to prevent the creation of a similar situation in Hungary. Hence Clages's mission—and the immediate creation in Budapest of a Jewish council. On this point the SS plan relies on observations made about the final solution in other European countries. The Jewish Council, very quickly set up by Wisliceny to convene in the grand consistory, must appear to be an institution of the Hungarian State; Regent Horthy himself will cover it with his authority. By this means will the distrust of the majority be put to rest. Then, Samuel Stern, "Crown Counselor," and president of the Jewish community, will meet with Nazis Krumey and Wisliceny, who will give him the respectful title of "Mr. Counselor." The effect will be multiple: the Jewish council feeds the illusion of a possible "collaboration," regroups the well-off and nationalistic Jews, saps the will to resist, and widens the gulf between ideas and generations. The "formula" has been pretested in Warsaw (with the *Judenrat*), in France (with the Union Générale des Israélites), and elsewhere.

The youth were right to be cautious, for, while reassuring negotiations are begun with the help of new Hungarian officials—such as Lazlo Endre and László Baky, the Interior State Secretary—Eichmann, with the help of other personalities, such as Peter Hein (Hungarian Gestapo) and László Ferenczy (gendarmerie), concerns himself with problems raised by the deportation to Auschwitz of Hungarian Jews *in their totality*. Another decision taken at the Majestic in the first days of the occupation deals with a conference of German railroad officials which will take place shortly in Vienna. Eichmann will attend the meeting, while one of his assistants remains in Budapest to study the first part of the trip with Hungarian railroad men. (He will have no difficulty finding all the help he needs.) Another matter of concern for model functionary Eichmann is the absorption capacity of the "mills"—that is, the gas chambers and the crematories. Without overlooking the official channels (he informs General Glucks), Eichmann makes contacts with Rudolf Höss, the commander of Auschwitz. He announces the approaching arrival of a "heavy load of Hungarians," and inquires about "accommodations." Höss's answer is to have a new railroad built, extending it to the very door of the gas chambers, and to quadruple his "death commandos."

Without even waiting for the results of the conferences, Eichmann initiates the first phase of deportation and extermination in the territory "to be cleaned out": the establishment of measures of discrimination and humiliation. "Everywhere and in every way, separate Jews from the Hungarians," recommends Ernst Kaltenbrunner, supreme chief of the Gestapo. From the wearing of the yellow star to the "regrouping" into camps near the stations, the program is worked out in detail. The idea is to break the spirit of the Jews, to separate them, to put the groups in opposition. The fear and famine that afflict Hungary, the constant spreading of anti-Semitic propaganda, put trump cards in the hands of the Nazis. There is no serious, organized opposition to fear.

"If everything goes as planned," concludes Eichmann as early as the second meeting in Budapest, "in less than six months we will announce to the Führer that the Jewish vermin of Hungary has been wiped out. It will be the fruition, the crowning of three years' effort, work, and thought. It will be another glorious page in the history of the Third Reich."

His assistants gone, Eichmann no doubt thinks that at last

he has the opportunity to rise in rank to SS Obersturmbannführer. In spite of the disastrous strategic situation presently facing the Third Reich, perhaps he even sees himself becoming a Standartenführer. From his window he contemplates Budapest at the bend of the Danube—beautiful, indolent city that has just given herself to the German army, so easily that the German-enacted curfew could be lifted, and on which the claws of the Nazi machine have closed. Beautiful city where Eichmann keeps a mistress (Madame Kutschera) and where he enjoys the cuisine, the varied and delicate wines, the sweet Torley champagne, the gypsy music, the taverns, and the nightclubs. A beautiful city in a beautiful country, which Eichmann prepares to "clean up" with the efficiency that three fruitful years' experience has provided him. A zealous functionary, he is satisfied and proud of the arrangements he has made. He controls them perfectly; he "senses" them down to the slightest gear within a gear. He is sure of the competence and standards of his subordinates. Nothing, he thinks, can put out of order the marvelous mechanism of death now being made ready.

His eye sweeps the left bank of the Danube—Pest, where the largest and the last Jewish community of occupied Europe lives—easy prey. Perhaps his eye grazes, without stopping, on the roof of a little house on Laudon Street, wrapped in shadow by the night. In its cellar the Hazalah partisans, near-children, sleep. Their combat plan is still but a dream. Yet it will block the most formidable man-killing machine that man has ever set into motion.

FOUR

Response to the Nazis: Hazalah

THESE ADVERSARIES—Eichmann and his acolytes would really laugh at them, had they the chance to be in their presence. Resistance fighters, these children whom no one takes seriously? Combatants, these ill-fed, clumsy kids, these skinny girls, these pious boys, lost in a daze, with their pale complexions? Partisans, these refugees, these orphans, these escapees from hell, these transplants, these sons without parents, these provincials ill-adapted to the capital? Terrorists, these youth with their feverish looks aimed toward the far-off hope of a Land one hundred times promised, and always taken back? These "pioneers" who can't live without prayers?

Among them there are more future rabbis, Talmudic students, future *tsaddicks* than "tough guys" used to handling guns and the tricks of the enemy. For every refugee or escaped prisoner, like Rafi Friedl or Zvi Goldfarb, there are as many seminary—or *yeshiva*—students, like Pinchas Rosenbaum, son of the rabbi of Kisvarda, or Emmeric Deutsch.

But these youth have their determination in common, and a plan. And that plan already has a name: *Hazalah*—"rescue." Significantly, this name is a contraction of "Waadat Ezar Vö-Hazalah Bö-Budapest," the name of the Jewish rescue committee of Budapest, which has been functioning for a year. Created originally to help the refugees from Slovakia and Poland, this committee is under the influence of the notable Zionists, Drs. Komoly and Kastner. Their work is intelligent, thoughtful, courageous, but dominated by one idea—to negotiate with the SS. All its initiatives are inspired by this illusion: the famous mission of Joël Brand in Turkey and Palestine will be developed within the committee—which also multiplies the contacts with SS leaders. The results of these dealings will be disastrous; only a handful of Jews will be saved—the 1,684 "samples" that the Nazis will lead in convoy toward Switzerland as proof of their good will, with a stopover in the "privileged" camp of Bergen-Belsen. After the war, the work of the committee and its policy of negotiation will give rise to sharp debate. Kastner's trial in Israel and his assassination shortly after the verdict of innocence will be the epilogue to this painful affair. (Today it appears clear, with the hindsight of history, that if the objectives of the committee were thoroughly humanitarian and honorable, the choice of the means and the negotiation were dramatic errors, even though they did not exclude the spirit of resistance.)

This error, the "young" Zionists feel instinctively and bear in anguish. For them, the search for dialogue, the hope for negotiation are only tragic illusions that lead to the acceptance of death. The elders—even Zionist elders, even those mandated by the Jewish Agency or the emigration groups—who grasp at any hope of negotiation with the SS are misguided—there is no discussion with death; one does not talk with the devil. The resources of Jewish dialectic, the possibilities of the spoken word, which so many generations have trusted, are weapons of the past. In the face of organized, industrial murder, in the face of a cold and organized enemy, the alternative offered to the Jews is imperative: to escape or to fight—even without arms. Any other option opens into the gas chamber.

To escape: even before the war, it was difficult to emigrate to Palestine; the British mandate authorities issued few certificates and those only to farmers. Since the opening of hostilities, the vigilance of Hadj Amin al Husseini, grand mufti of Jerusalem, zealous personal friend of Hitler, has increased steadily; escape networks through Bulgaria and Rumania are fragile and precarious. How long will they hold out?

To fight: there are many ways of fighting.

Among the Hachomer Hazair, refugees like Rafi Friedl, who has known many camps, think they can foresee how the Nazi plan will unfold; they will begin in the provinces, regrouping the Jews in ghettos, then into transfer camps near railroads. They will act quickly to take advantage of the mental confusion and the lack of information. Only after that will they take on the big cities. And in the end, Budapest—in three or four months.

Simultaneously, as tokens to feed false hopes, they will liberate a few arrested Jews; they will seek allies among the Jews themselves through vain promises. Warsaw furnishes the example: there, in the beginning, the Jewish Council itself designated the victims for deportation. The Jewish police escorted the condemned up to the assembly point. Then one day the police assigned to deliver a quota of deportees had to turn in their own families. The experience accumulated by the Nazis in the already "cleaned" countries of Europe will keep them from fumbling and making errors. The development of the military situation will push them to accelerate the process to the maximum. (This view of the problem will prove to be correct: in Hungary, the program was accelerated, every phase of the "clean up" shortened, and delays practically eliminated.)

But this analysis of the situation is not, unfortunately, shared by the Hungarians. Only one course of action is possible: alert the Jews in the provinces, enlighten them on the situation, and also give them the means to thwart the regrouping. It cannot be a question of resistance or combat. The Jews of the provinces, pious, indolent, frightened, and generally mystical, are not partisans. Even if they were, there would be no way to arm them. The only hope consists in "Magyarizing" them, in removing them from their own surroundings, village or town, where they are too well known, too easy to spot; in providing them with Aryan identities; and, however possible, in melting them into the mass of the country. To awaken them, to make them conscious of the risks weighing upon them, to convince them to leave their homes, abandon their synagogues, their *yeshivas,* to come under the protection of false identities, and melt into the anonymity of big towns, if possible Budapest. Where can one better hide than in the crowd! The difficulty of this task is immense—psychologically and technically. But there is no other solution. From this perspective, the young Hazalah Zionists set out to create new, clandestine presses. At this stage of the fight the principal weapon is the false ID card. The first messengers who will take the great risk of leaving for the provinces will be furnished with them, for themselves and for the families they will attempt to save.

Yet neither is the military aspect of the Hazalah plan neglected. As any wide-scale insurrection is beyond the Hungarian Zionists, their strategy tends toward a line of secret defenses, caches and bunkers, where the rare arms they possess or succeed in getting will be stored. Combat, armed insurrection, constitute the ultimate decision. They will have recourse to it only after they have exhausted all other possibilities. They will fight without any hope of survival, for the chances in case of confrontation will be practically zero. They will fight only to have some choice as to how they die.

The rush of events will confirm the foresight of the young Hazalahs and push them to speed up even further the execution of their plan in the face of an active, hurried enemy; the very day the Hungarian Nazis seize power, the arrests, rumors of which have been going the rounds since morning, are confirmed. Others follow. During the night a raid takes place in the Schwabenberg sector, where Eichmann has set up his operations. All the wealthy Jews living in villas are arrested with their families. They had thought themselves protected by powerful Hungarian friendships; no one will hear of them again.

In the following days, arrests multiply; the Hungarian cabinet enacts a first series of ordinances applicable to the whole territory; the obligatory wearing of the yellow star comes accompanied by a flood of prohibitions: against changing residence, against taking a train, a boat, against using taxicabs, keeping a bank account, a radio. On the streetcars, the Jews have the right only to the rear car. Jewish doctors can treat only Jews; Jewish engineers, pharmacists, publicists, actors must cease their activities immediately. Telephone service for Jews is suspended. Practicing the Jewish religion and kosher butchering, as well as Talmudic education, are forbidden.

The brutality and the rapidity of putting these measures into effect leave no room for doubt; it is indeed immobilization, a prelude to regrouping, to deportation, and to death. The youth of Hazalah know this, while the townspeople pretend to see in these measures an end, not a beginning, and continue, on the basis of the multiplication of "contacts," to nourish the hope of an accommodation, of a negotiated peace with the SS.

FIVE

The Sacred Scrolls

AMID ALL the upsetting news of the first days of the occupation, one thing especially gives the religious Jews of Budapest, young or old, a feeling of disaster: the SS occupation of the city's two consistories. This immediate and brutal action seems ominous not so much for the future as for the precise risk it lays on the upcoming celebration of *Pesach*—Passover.

The great feast commemorating the exodus of the Jews from Egypt is to begin in two weeks. The only bread pious Jews can eat during this time is matzo, an unleavened bread baked under the supervision of a rabbi which commemorates the dough dried in the sun during the exodus. The matzo is ready, stored in the cellars of the Orthodox consistory on Dob Street; it is out of the question to replenish the stock in so short a time, or to find, because of stricter and stricter rationing, additional flour.

The leaders of the Orthodox community hold a meeting, as early as Monday, to study the problem. Against all logic, they decide to risk an action in order to recover the matzo and distribute it to the pious families of Budapest and its suburbs. But what action? After much hesitation they decide in favor of an operation combining bluff, legality, and guile. Emile Deutsch, a prominent lawyer in the community, is commissioned to take the matter in his hands; like many cultivated Hungarian Jews, he speaks German without an accent, is in possession of a whole set of papers in German (he often tries cases in Vienna), and his physical appearance is well suited for impressing the occupying authority.

Unconscious (or voluntarily neglectful) of the enormous risks involved in such proceedings, Deutsch presents himself on Monday morning at the consistory and hands the sentry his card written in German. He announces that he wishes to meet the officer in charge immediately.

"For what reasons?"

"A matter concerning the consistory," answers Deutsch with all the impatience of a German Herr Doktor.

The sentry vanishes, then comes back under orders to show the visitor into the "office" occupied since yesterday by the SS Sturmbahnführer Bombolovsky.

A curious dialogue takes place. Stating his identity, his religion, and the motive for his visit, Deutsch insists on the important role matzo plays in the celebration of the Jewish Easter. The SS officer listens patiently, in silence. Deutsch thinks he has failed. And that his chances of leaving the consistory a free man are rather slim. Can one seriously imagine, at this stage of the war, an SS dignitary lending an ear to the claims of a Jew—especially on a point of religious law? However, a polite statement issues from the Nazi's mouth:

"But we too have a need for this bread!"

Astounded, the lawyer grasps at this opportunity for a dialogue. He answers that flour is not lacking in Hungary—

especially for the German troops—while the pious Jews of Budapest would desperately miss the matzo. That, everything considered, the officer could at small cost accomplish a good deed—and eventually do some "business."

"All right," Bombolovsky cuts in. "Granted! I'll give you back the bread. At no charge."

"Thank you," answers the lawyer. "But that's not all. We'd also like to put the sacred scrolls of the tabernacle in a safe place . . ."

Later, Deutsch explains that this request, which had not been anticipated, or hardly mentioned, came almost spontaneously to his lips. Since the German was accepting a discussion, why not take full advantage of it?

"The sacred scrolls?"

"Let me show you. They are down in the synagogue."

The Nazi and the lawyer—one preceding the other—come before the tabernacle. Here are kept the parchment scrolls on which, generation upon generation, scribes have calligraphed the Pentateuch. There are about 50 scrolls, in their velvet covers embroidered with threads of gold and silver, heavy with many ornaments of precious metal. Surprised, the Nazi looks alternately at the scrolls and at the lawyer, who is motionless. Finally he breaks the silence:

"All right, you can have the scrolls too—but I keep the ornaments. Anyway you won't be keeping them long; all Jewish goods will soon be seized. Come back tomorrow!"

During the night the pious Jews discuss things at length. Some think that it is a trap; the SS will not give either the bread or the Torah!

At any rate, at dawn the next day a dozen Jews present themselves at the consistory with Emile Deutsch. They do not take with them any young people capable of upsetting the Nazis. The matzo is ready in the courtyard. Enigmatically, ominously, Bombolovsky stands next to the sacred scrolls.

"Take them. Hurry!"

The Jews take the scrolls out of their covers. Some SS watch them. When the Jews appear in the courtyard with their precious load, they find that the SS soldiers occupying the consistory are at attention, forming a kind of double guard of honor. Led by the officer, the pious Jews proceed through the soldiers and find themselves in the street. Many among them fear some macabre spectacle; they expect the worst. They know that the Nazis have a sadistic taste for blending formalism and violence. The day before, old men had been forced to "dance," keeping time in the street, then to form a lane, before being set free. Soldiers pulled the beards of rabbis, threatening to set them on fire. Afterwards all the Jews had to execute the Hitlerian salute. In their murderous madness, the Nazis often seize the opportunity to conduct some travesty of a ritual.

But the SS officer doesn't give the order to fire. He shakes hands with the lawyer, while the bearers hurriedly take their leave.

"Sincerely," says Deutsch, "I thank you."

Bombolovsky wears a bizarre smile.

"Don't thank me. I'm going to explain the reasons for my gesture. I have more Jewish blood on my hands than you might think. Not too long ago, I was at Drohovic in the Ukraine. Our mission was to deport the whole Jewish population of the town. A routine mission. We led the group toward the railroad cars. At the tail end of the procession, an old rabbi was dragging along; a corporal was beating him with the butt of his rifle. I ordered him to stop; something in this weighed-down old Jew moved me. I don't know what; I'm not a soft-hearted person. The old man raised his eyes to me and I read in them gratitude as well as pity. It lasted a fraction of a second. I forgot the incident. The convoy of Jews left. Forty-eight hours later, with my detachment I fell into an ambush laid by partisans. Everybody around me died—and I didn't have a scratch. A true miracle. Let me show you . . ."

He takes a picture out of his wallet: a military vehicle totally wrecked. He remains silent a moment:

"You find this absurd, don't you, Herr Doktor? But to this day I'm convinced I owe my salvation to the old rabbi's grateful look. That's why I gave you the matzo, and the sacred scrolls. It is payment for my life. Don't thank me. Good-bye."

Emile Deutsch in his turn leaves, thoughtful.

It is March 22, 1944. (Almost all the sacred scrolls of the Budapest community are now in Israel.) For the pious Jews of Budapest it is a fervent Passover. For many of them it is to be their last. Their prayers and their thoughts are raised toward God who had permitted this feast, but they stop a moment to celebrate the memory of a Ukrainian rabbi who died in a gas chamber.

SIX

Missions to the Provinces

DURING THE last days of March, the Jewish Council begins to function and establishes itself in the premises of the grand consistory.

The young Zionists can do nothing to oppose what they interpret as an illusory form of collaboration with the Nazis. Everything takes place beyond their reach, in a world not their own. They sense a trap. They measure its effects. But nobody pays any attention to their protests.

At the head of the council the Nazis put Counselor Samuel Stern, whose reputation for integrity is considerable in Budapest. Among the eight members, only one is a Zionist, the lawyer Nisson-Kahan. The role of the Jewish Council is to "maintain order," "to keep the peace"—Nazi order and the peace of near death. Deaf to the protests and adjurations of the young, Counselor Stern decides immediately to deliver large sums of cash, paintings, ancient books, and precious pianos to the SS. Komoly, a Jewish hero of World War I and a Zionist of the moderate wing, takes charge of tightening the contacts that the council fosters with some important Hungarian Nazis. As for Dr. Kastner, in conjunction with the activity of the council, he negotiates with Becher, an SS officer who seems willing to let himself be convinced. Each of them will achieve some results—very meager results—for the watchword among the SS is to give minimal tokens, to feed the illusion of possible accord, in order to divide the Jews and make them more vulnerable. And also to collect eventual tokens for the postwar period at little cost and without damage to the priority mission of extermination. (In the end, some of them will succeed in this juggling act. Becher, the "good, corrupted SS" saved his skin and now lives in Germany.)

The Hazalah partisans, more than other young people, are conscious that their elders blindly imprison themselves in the subtle and complex network that the diabolical SS weaves around them.

"Don't you understand what they are up to?" a partisan one day asks his father, a one-time Budapest wholesaler, who is in favor of the Jewish Council.

"There is no choice! The Resistance offers us no chance. And that's not the way we live."

It is a conflict of ideas, but also of generations. The young don't believe in the "good SS." They despise the Jewish Council. They place all their hopes in their own plan for action. But they also know that if this plan has little chance to succeed in the face of the Nazis, it has none at all of convincing the "lukewarms" of the Jewish Council. And in addition to the anguish of an uncertain future, they feel the disappointment and sadness of being misunderstood and rejected by their elders.

A situation all the more paradoxical in that, from the first days following the Nazi occupation and the start of the sinister bargaining between the Jews and the SS, the young Zionists' Hazalah plan, on one precise and surprising point, seems to give rise to a gleam of hope. Eager to take advantage of every opportunity, of the slightest imperfection in the death machine they are facing, ready to cling to any "hold" they can get their hands on, the partisans analyze the situation they now have to deal with.

Soon, the idea comes to them to circulate a great number of false ID cards, as a means of creating confusion at the administrative level. The Nazis, working statistically, count on the extermination of a certain number of Jews. It is reported that in Denmark the Nazis were held in check because *all the Danes* declared themselves Jews. Such a movement of solidarity being inconceivable among the Hungarians, the opposite situation will be presented to them: far fewer Jews than expected.

Polish and Slovakian refugees who had been caught up in concentration-camp logic and who, miraculously, escaped it were all struck by one fact: like every German system, the Nazi death machine is founded upon order and method. It is a huge structure which attacks from the outside can only scratch. Perhaps, however, it is *vulnerable from the inside.* It is a heavy industry, a colossal mechanism without flexibility, which a defect, no matter how minor, could impede. The massive appearance of false IDs, upsetting the forecasts, could spoil some of the Nazis' plans. Of course, all the Jews wouldn't be saved—but it would be throwing a monkey wrench into the machinery. And soon, some creaking can be heard. The Hungarian gendarmerie, the Nazis' zealous servants, are thrown into confusion. They are missing Jews here and there. The Nazis become impatient—which might be interpreted as an encouraging sign.

Informed of the reactions that their maneuver provokes

among the enemy, the young concentrate even more on the fabrication of these false documents. In Budapest itself, as early as the end of March, more than 20 underground printing plants are running. Transport and distribution of false IDs in the provinces, now that travel prohibitions have been imposed upon the Jews, call for difficult but essential missions. Many messengers, many carriers will be arrested and shot down by the gendarmerie or the Nazi police. Many will get through and succeed in establishing contacts with communities far from the endangered capital.

Within each movement, there is an appeal for volunteers; almost all the partisans respond. Among dozens of such volunteers is one Pinchas Rosenbaum, 20 years old, of the B'ni Akiba. In order to travel more easily and pass through police checkpoints, he has adopted the costume and manners of a young Hungarian seminarian; as for personal papers, he has a streetcar commutation card, the only national document on which religion does not appear. His mission takes him to Kisvarda. His family lives there. As much as possible, the movement sends its messengers into towns and regions they know, places of which they are natives. Like the other pious Jews of the community, like tens of thousands of Jews in Hungary, Pinchas's parents live in ignorance of the danger threatening them. His father is the town's rabbi, and a descendant of Loew, the legendary grand rabbi of Prague, the architect of the Golem. His mother, his five brothers and sisters are extremely pious.

Pinchas has crossed the dangerous checkpoints of the Pest station. In the train, while approaching Kisvarda, anxiety and doubt seize him; has he the right to trouble his parents' souls on the eve of Passover, when they are joyfully preparing the celebration of God's justice, which permitted the end of slavery in Egypt? Is he entitled to throw upon the luminous world of faith and love the hideous shadows of deportation and extermination?

Pinchas hesitates. And all over the country hundreds of young messengers, charged with this impossible mission of information, of "awakening," hesitate as he does.

In any case, Pinchas thinks, even if he succeeds in convincing them, he won't get his parents to accept the solution advocated in Budapest. His father, the rabbi, will never leave his synagogue, his faithful; he will never agree to slip into the identity of a Christian, to disguise himself, to eat non-kosher food, to miss the holy Friday-evening service. . . . Pinchas suddenly realizes that the preceding generation will never truly understand. The real tragedy, however, is that the younger generation will not want to break with their elders. What will then become of these young men who nevertheless are not willing to surrender and who must save themselves? Pinchas will address himself to them. He'll persuade them to leave their town—where everybody knows them—to melt, with false identities, into the anonymity of Budapest.

And in fact, in bribing a printer in Kisvarda, Pinchas will manage to have enough false IDs made to provide for almost all the youth of the community. He doesn't offer one to his father; he simply celebrates the Passover festivities fervently at his side. But in the evening, when the youngest of his brothers asks, according to the tradition, the first of the four ritual questions: "How is this night different from all other nights . . . ?" the eyes of everyone there meet and fill with tears.

When he leaves the little town, his mission is accomplished: he has distributed the false IDs to all those who are in a position to use them. He feels he will never see his parents again. But he feels, too, when he receives his father's blessing, that nothing can break the ties that link his generation to these pious Jews and their fate. The wrench is excruciating. Why this sacrifice, why this fatality? Where is God's design in it? For Pinchas, a deeply religious boy—and ardently militant—it is an anguished journey. Today, having survived, he credits God's will for not having yielded then to abandonment, to despair.

In all the provincial communities, the other Hazalah envoys accomplish the same mission and endure the same wrench. At Cluj, in Transylvania, the partisans are even called blasphemers and are ejected from the town; the head of the community calls God's malediction upon them and declares to his faithful: "Stop your ears against the impious talk of these young people! The All-High will never let our community of the just perish!" Elsewhere a wise man states: "We don't need you because the war will be over in a few weeks. We know this from the Cabala—and also because the amount of our suffering cannot be surpassed."

For many messengers, boys or girls, whose proposals and false IDs are refused in indignation, the separation is heartbreaking.

"We knew that our parents in the provinces were lost! It was as though we had abandoned them to an invisible fire. . . ."

Bela Grunwalt—Coça—of the moderate wing, must, sick at heart, endure the accusations of his father:

"You are a liar," he says. "I'll tell the consistory to keep the Jews from listening to your rubbish. You are confusing souls and you create panic! We are putting our trust in the government of Hungary. They'll know how to protect us. You say you are Zionist. Hasn't Kallay, the former prime minister, granted, even recently, legal existence to the Zionist Federation?"

Back in Budapest, the messengers—those who have gotten past the police at least—can do nothing but draw up the balance sheet of their too-meager action. How many of the mass of endangered, condemned Hungarian Jews have agreed to go underground? Very few, too few . . . And this refusal is not characteristic of provincial Jews only; the attitude it reveals exists in Budapest too. Moshe Weiskopf, for instance, wastes his energy in vain efforts to keep the Jews of the capital from wearing the yellow star. He himself has been living for a year under a false identity. But his example, for the most part, raises the Jews' mistrust. One of them whom he tried to convince ejected him, saying:

"To wear the star of King David is an honor! Aren't you ashamed to want to deprive us of this joy?"

On his rounds, Weiskopf wears a leather jacket, military boots, and a cap to which is affixed a badge suggesting the Arrow Cross. He is reproached for this attire that enables him to walk the city streets:

"A Hungarian Jew has no right to dress like that!"

The Hazalah partisans, boys and girls, exchanging their uneasy talk, measure the abyss that separates Hungarian Judaism from the reality of things—an abyss that thousands and thousands of dead will soon fill. But in this blindness, in this suicidal refusal, they also derive new strength for their mission.

SEVEN

Liquidated Ghettos

WHY REFUSE to admit the obvious? As had happened in other Jewish communities of Europe, the Hungarian community is already beginning to feel the pangs of death. Its days are numbered. The itineraries are cleared; the trains are formed on paper. In a few weeks—perhaps sooner—the Hungarian Jews will experience the horrors of transportation in sealed cars, the selection on the camp platforms, the walk to the shower rooms, which are now known as gas chambers. Then the slow asphyxiation, the horror of a death without reason. Rumor has it that some death camps, situated too close to the Eastern front, have been dismantled by the executioners. Tanks have leveled the ground after the barracks and installations are destroyed. On the scene of their crimes, the Nazis have planted grass. When the liberators reach the site of the vanished camp, not a single detail in the terrain, not a single vestige will enable them to locate it. Such, in fact, was the Nazi plan, partially carried out at Treblinka. It is also said that the engineers of the Reich have perfected a new, even more efficient gas. And some, on the strength of mysterious information, go so far as to assert that German doctors practice dreadful experiments on Jewish prisoners before executing them. This rumor, it must be said, arouses only incredulity; in such a time of doubt and anguish, so sensitive to "propaganda," in such a vacuum of information, where hearsay is distorted, swelled beyond belief, an assertion like this sounds more like the false news the enemy circulates than like the testimony of survivors.

"Experiments on living prisoners? I forbid you to spread such stupid rumors . . . you're putting yourself at the level of the Nazis and their base propaganda."

This is the answer one young Misrahi boy gets from his uncle, a one-time functionary in Budapest.

And when he tells of the measures that sweep down on the Jews in the provinces as a prelude to their approaching deportation, he is utterly crushed by this response: "Never mind the provinces! Here, in Budapest, we are protected. . . ."

Thoughtlessness, selfishness, blind obedience? Who will ever analyze the multiple components of that kind of attitude? Nonetheless, the action against the Jews has begun, violent, precise, methodical—and already near. A few miles from Budapest—and all the way to the borders—the Hungarian gendarmerie and, occasionally, German executioners from special commandos and some members of the SS are in charge of arresting the Jews scattered in villages, market towns, and small cities. The military and the police cordon a street or a district, knock down the doors, and enter Jewish houses, howling and shouting:

"*Raus!* Out!"

Sometimes the unfortunate, caught in bed, at work, or even at prayer, haven't the time to grab a suitcase or a bag. They are huddled together in trucks. Some of them witness the looting of their homes. They are ordered to take all their money with them, all the jewels they possess. They are also told that if any valuable is discovered after their departure, their whole family will be executed on the spot. There are many cases of executions in the trucks, or along the road. The old, the sick, the small children have to strain to keep up, to hoist themselves without help onto the trucks. Those who fail, or seem to show too little willingness to obey orders, are cruelly beaten. Old men are forced to crawl in the mud; the Hungarian gendarmes split their sides laughing at such a performance. Rabbis are forced to pull down their pants and execute a kind of grotesque dance to the sound of music; those who do not dance are clubbed by the gendarmes. They cut the "earlocks"—the sideburns—of pious Jews and even, in many places, set the beards of old men on fire. . . .

The non-Jewish Hungarians show no reaction. One can even see peasants helping the police knocking down doors and pointing out possible caches. Denunciations pour forth, motivated by the lure of looting, of dividing up the land or the houses. For one act of mutual aid or mercy (priests agreed to take in and hide Jewish children when the rumor of an imminent pogrom reached the village), there are a thousand scenes of cruelty and sadism. For the great roundup of "their" Jews, the Hungarians lend a hand to the assassins.

These accounts and the details accompanying them fail to shake the quietude and confidence of the Budapest Jews. The young partisans are dumbfounded. At the Laudon Street Misrahi, they lose hope of ever communicating their feeling of defiance to the others, if not their wish to fight. Don't they understand? Or do they refuse to understand?

Sadness, anguish for the future, but also unshakable will to stand up to the enemy! And through this night, already, like the shimmering flame of a candle, comes a tiny gleam of victory; astonished not to find at home (since they cannot move) all the Jews listed in the Hungarian Registrar General (which they obtained with no difficulty), the Nazis sense an opposition. This is the first result of the distribution of false identities. There are Jews missing in the death roll, unexplainable absences, disappearances. From reliable sources we know that reports were sent to Budapest, that Nazi agents in the provinces asked for reinforcements. A certain uneasiness sprouts up among the Hungarian Nazis; they still refuse to admit they are facing an organization, but they foresee problems. Are the Hungarian Jews going to be finicky now about letting themselves be deported? This idea, contrary to "racist" theories, nonetheless occurs to them for the first time, in Budapest—even before the end of March.

This is certainly the reason why a torrent of ordinances and decrees, meant to paralyze the Jewish population, will flood the country in the next few days. And why the volume will be recorded in the press, always obedient to the Nazis; the major Hungarian newspapers, from then on, ceaselessly demand ever more severe and urgent chastisement of the Jews, "allies of the Bolsheviks," responsible for all the bombardment and all the misfortunes of Hungary in general. For the young Zionists, this parallel acceleration of concrete measures and condemnations is proof that the Nazis are ready to proceed to the final stage of their action—and that the beginning of the operation in Budapest itself is near.

Hungarian citizenship is withdrawn from the Jews; in the provinces, Jews are herded into ghettos. The wearing of the yellow star, the first of the measures enacted, is now codified by decree 1240; the star is mandatory from the age of six on, with no distinction of sex. The badge must be four inches high and four inches wide, securely sewn on, even on work clothes, and *worn at home*. The cafés, pastry shops, cigar stores, public baths are closed to Jews throughout the country; they are no longer allowed to go from one place to another (bicycles and streetcars are forbidden them) . The food rations for the Jews are limited to a quarter pound of meat a week and three-quarters of a pound of sugar a month. Jews are no longer entitled to the allotments of fat, paprika, or poppy seeds. In any case, going out before 1 P.M. is prohibited them—and at that time of the day, the stores have long been emptied, even in Budapest.

The actual regrouping is very soon enacted in the capital; in Budapest, the "Jewish houses," future prisons, begin to be designated by big painted Stars of David. In the face of the menacing situation, the partisans work without respite, offering false Christian papers, advising families to change districts, to refuse the regrouping, and urging the young to melt into the crowd.

On April 3, Budapest is subjected to violent air bombardment; in full daylight, in successive waves, American planes pour a rain of bombs onto industrial sectors of the city and the outskirts. At Pestsentlörinc the oil refineries and a number of factories are in flames. Many apartment buildings are damaged as well and, in the days that follow, the authorities have to face a rehousing problem. The *Evening News* naturally imputes responsibility for this bombing to the Jews, and immediately an ordinance stipulates that homeless victims be relocated in Jewish apartments in Budapest. When informed of this ordinance, Eichmann gives his approval to the Hungarian Gestapo; such regroupings go according to his immediate plans. After a second bombardment, this time by night, Eichmann will insist that more than a thousand Jewish apartments be made available at once. The expelled will be huddled together, 15 to one room, in selected houses.

Among the partisans, meetings take place every day to

assess the situation. The fabrication and circulation of false IDs and the establishment of liaison with other resistance groups are intensified. Partisans are alerted in the provinces, others at the borders, in the M.U.S.Z. (labor battalions), on the farms, in Budapest. These conscious, courageous elements, ready for resistance, must be localized, accessible in case of emergency. Liaison is a vital problem. Shelters are provided in the country; Hungary needs farmworkers (Pauli, under a Christian cover for a year, has become a specialist in this kind of work). Dependable, combative partisans are placed wherever they have a chance to escape the raids.

The Tijoul plans for escape take shape. New connections are established. Emissaries have been successful in crossing and recrossing the Rumanian border several times. Rafi Friedl is at work. The creation of bunkers and caches is also in progress. Zvi Goldfarb trains an enthusiastic and wary group; several places have been located on Buda hilltops and around the city. Secret observation posts are set up, from which the young Zionists will be able to watch closely the movements of Nazi detachments in the city and signal their approach. It is already the first draft of a military organization. There are a few arms, mainly automatic pistols bought from deserters. The supply is minuscule, but the Zionist resistance is no longer totally unarmed; the weapons are greased, maintained, scattered in safe caches. Every night, in cellars, "instructors" teach the partisans the handling of arms and street combat. Their morale is amazing.

The messenger network is functioning. Young boys like David Auslander, girls like Haga Blum or Pnina, are volunteers, in spite of the risks, for all the liaison missions in Budapest, in the suburbs, and in the provinces. Under the nose of the police, they continue to distribute false IDs to those who have decided to go underground, and offer hiding places to those who refuse to let themselves be counted, regrouped, and concentrated; they work at convincing others, in spite of police surveillance, ceaseless identity checks, risks of denunciation—in contempt of laws and ordinances.

Operation Hazalah has started. Documents seized after the war show that the Hungarian Nazis and German counter-espionage, though aware of the existence of an organized force standing in the way of their plans, never gathered the elements for a serious evaluation of the adversary. The Nazis underestimated the resistance that was taking shape. On March 31, Veesenmayer, the true gauleiter of Hungary, writes to Ribbentrop: "The Hungarian government proves itself serious and acts in its fight against the Jewish enemy at an unbeatable speed."

When this report arrives in Berlin, Hazalah's first military "bunker" is completed; Zvi Goldfarb, who lives under the identity of an Italian worker, Mario Marchesi, has managed to rent an isolated villa a few miles from Budapest. The owners quickly understood what use these young "foreigners" intended for their place, but they did not object; on the contrary, they assured the tenants of their cooperation. With his wife, Neska, and some ten partisans, Goldfarb has dug a second basement. An invisible trapdoor leads to the cellar. A complicated system provides for ventilation and the intake and evacuation of water. In this bunker, the partisans will soon store their most precious weapons—and their only machine gun. The idea that their movement is now in possession of organized caches, even mock ones and usable only for a handful of people, is comforting to the Zionists. A liaison network ready to take any risk, hidden bases, false ID printing plants, perilous escape connections, a few weapons, and an immense, shared willpower: it is already more than the first draft of a resistance.

EIGHT

The Labor Camps

SOMETIMES THERE is no better asylum than in the bosom of the enemy. . . . That is what many young Zionists think now, at the beginning of May, as they turn over in their pockets the documents that enroll them in the "Compulsory Labor Service," the M.U.S.Z.—and that summon them, upon receipt, to the centers assigned them. The first reaction among the Hazalah partisans is, of course, refusal. The M.U.S.Z. has a terrible reputation. If going underground is to become imperative, inevitable, why not plunge into it right away instead of joining the Hungarian camps? This would only mean advancing the date of fighting, beginning the combat in darkness earlier than planned.

On reflection, some youths have discovered that to obey the law might offer a better protection—for the moment.

After all, it would be just another paradox in the situation of the young Jews of Hungary.

The important thing is not to make mistakes. Hazalah is an audacious and fragile enterprise. All its objectives, all the plans for action and resistance that have been built up rest on tight analyses. The margin for tolerable error is narrow, if not nonexistent. As one of the young leaders has put it: "We have almost nothing to fight with. Only our determination to fight. We are both the combatants and the weapons!"

Is there a fault, a defect in the labor service, the M.U.S.Z. of evil memory? Does a means of taking advantage of it exist? Before answering negatively, the groups study the problem in detail. And the partisans reach a curious conclusion.

Since 1939 a Hungarian law has excluded Jews from military service, a major insult in a country where valor in war has always been considered a fundamental feature of the national character. Barred from glory, theoretical glory, Hungarian Jews old enough to carry arms were assigned, after 1939, to labor service, a kind of hard labor in civilian clothes—a yellow brassard on the left arm (white for converted Jews), and a military cap without the green, white, and red cockade, the Hungarian national colors. Their battalions are under the command of career non-commissioned officers, reserve officers, non-commissioned reserve officers, and recruits suddenly promoted to the rank of corporal, under the command of warrant officers. From the start the Jewish labor conscripts have been subjected to an absurd discipline and, in the different camps where they were assembled, have been made victims of abusive authority on the part of irresponsible, brutal, sadistic chiefs slaking vague social grudges. If the treatment endured by the young Jews was merely rigorous as long as their regiment was inside Hungary, it became simply unbearable in the Ukraine in 1941, after Hungary entered the war on the side of the Germans against Russia.

Thinking they were flying to the aid of victory, the Bardossy government threw itself into the war a few days after the beginning of Operation Barbarossa; the old animosity of the Hungarian toward the Slavs awoke violently. (The memory of the excesses of Bela Kun's Red Guard invaders was still alive in Hungary: there wasn't a child who didn't know that the great national poet Petöfi had perished with his chest pierced by a Cossack's lance!) Caught in this dubious situation, the labor regiments of young Jews soon became entangled in the "operations"; all the more so because the Hungarian army, underequipped and not mobile, soon met serious setbacks in occupied Soviet territories.

More than 40,000 Hungarian Jews of the M.U.S.Z. were to die in 1941 and 1942 beyond the borders of their country, mainly in the Ukraine, the battle and occupation field assigned by the Germans to the Hungarians. Those young Jews—who didn't wear "uniforms" (contrary to what Hannah Arendt,* ill-informed on this point as well, later contended)—died, victims not only of mine-clearing operations as cruel as they were useless, but also of the harshness of the Hungarians commanding them. Among all the dramatic events that occurred in the destiny of the Hungarian Jew, that was one of the most dramatic. Deprived of victory, more and more threatened by the resistant—and sometimes even attacking—Red Army, the Hungarian officers of this weaponless expeditionary corps avenged their humiliations on their own men (whose enthusiasm as warriors was, of course, relative at best).

Brutalities, shootings, summary executions, and torture succeeded one another, imparting a sense of domination, of victory at small cost and without risk over unfortunate unarmed men. Starving, defenseless, they were suddenly called

* In her book *Eichmann in Jerusalem, A Report* (New York, Viking Press, 1963).

traitors, spies, Communists, Bolsheviks, enemies. The patchwork attire of the young Jewish workers, their too-light civilian clothing in rags (they were not entitled to receive either packages or mail from their families), their pitiful appearance, exasperated even more the quasi-religious hatred. Some survivors, who later managed to return to Budapest and join the Hazalah partisans, told how, in that godforsaken land, in the forests and marshes of the Ukraine, where Soviet partisans prowled, the discovery of vestiges of Jewish communities already destroyed by the Nazis, of synagogues turned into warehouses or stables, of profaned Jewish cemeteries, seemed to act upon the Hungarian cadre as so many incitements for hatred and violence. One evening a regiment of exhausted young Jews arrived at Berditchev, the town of Levi Isaac and of Baal Sem Tov, the founder of Hasidism. By chance they came upon the site of the old community cemetery behind the railroad; the old graves had been ransacked, the tombstones with their inscriptions pulverized. The cemetery had provided the latrines for the occupying Germans! Silence, the silence of death, brooded over the town, which in the past had been a shrine of Hasidic Judaism. On orders, the labor conscripts scattered among the abandoned and burned-down houses in search of shelter for the night. In the morning, mustering the men, a Hungarian officer noticed the presence of a five- or six-year-old child, a little Ukrainian Jew who had miraculously escaped the massacre by hiding in the corner of a cellar. Terrorized, alone in the enemy-populated town, gnawed by hunger and despair, he had emerged. A boy from the M.U.S.Z. had given him a piece of his bread. He was now asleep, tiny, pale, unreal—but smiling. The Hungarian officer looked at him a moment, then gave a boy the order to deliver the child to a German patrol.

"But they'll kill him!"

"That's right. We might as well kill him ourselves."

And the officer killed the sleeping little Jew with one shot from his revolver.

Thousands of similar scenes stand out as milestones in the epic of labor service in the Ukraine; the survivors were unable to utter without a shudder the names of the martyred towns—Berditchev, Ostrogorsk and its death forest, Stavi-Ostrol, Dovnitsa Dorosits. In the last, 800 Hungarian Jewish conscripts, all of them sick, were assembled in a barn and burned alive. Those who attempted to flee were shot down with machine guns—by their own Hungarian officers. . . . Elsewhere, in 20-below weather, they were showered with water and abandoned, by night, without shelter.

If the survivors of the M.U.S.Z., miraculously back from the Ukraine (there was hope, against all logic, that other Jews had been taken prisoner by the Russians and would return after the war, and that hope lasted a long time), told terrible, discouraging stories, the telling of which intensified in the partisans the desire for revenge, for fighting the Nazis, other youths presented a different picture. These were the conscripts who had performed their labor service in Hungary.

At the time that their comrades at the front were encountering hatred and horror, they were assembled in camps and barracks, getting almost the same food as the soldiers of the regular army, and as a whole under the same, but not so strict, discipline.

Their descriptions were of tremendous interest to the heads of Hazalah. In the camps inside the country, working conditions were indeed harsh but acceptable. The conscripts were officered by Hungarian military men whose main ambition was to keep their homefront jobs, therefore not to attract the attention of their superiors. From the end of 1942, warrant officers were recruited among redrafted, older men, closer to civilian life than their opposite numbers of the M.U.S.Z.

beyond the borders. They thought less of persecuting the young Jews placed under their authority than of returning as soon as possible to their families and jobs. Their zeal was moderate; every punishment inflicted upon a conscript had to be the subject of a report in military form. They didn't feel, as the cadre did in the Ukraine, that they held the power of life and death, a feeling fostered by distance, the state of war, and the absence of laws and regulations. In Hungary, their anti-Semitism was muffled. Cases have been cited of non-commissioned officers who completely changed personalities when they crossed the borders of their country, with their platoons or units of Jewish workers. One Ukraine escapee told the story of a certain sergeant major named Varga who, leading a group through the Carpathians about a mile from the border, suddenly pulled out his revolver and shouted: "Wait till we get out of the country, and I'll shoot every one of you!" The same sergeant later managed to organize useless missions—the transport of heavy pieces to the tops of icy mountains—to give himself the opportunity in the mountain wilderness to quietly assassinate dozens of Jewish conscripts. When his officers became concerned or regarded these operations as useless and denied him these special "commandos," the sergeant major became so frustrated that he had a nervous breakdown and in the end requested a transfer to a combat unit. But, on national territory, this type of noncom, who indulged in assassination for its own sake, didn't exist, or at least could not reveal his true self openly. It was therefore possible to survive and even to organize in spite of the labor-camp discipline.

The reports of those who have gone through this experience confirm it. In Hungary, the morale of the M.U.S.Z. conscripts who work in quarries digging antitank trenches, or strengthening fortifications is excellent. "Victory is near," they say. "We'll be home in September, in time for Rosh

Hashanah and Yom Kippur!" And the Hazalah leaders quickly come to the conclusion that the partisan who is called, or on the point of being called, should obey the draft notice, since service is now carried on inside the national borders. For the present—and for some time to come—this solution offers, within the terms of the resistance plan, a certain number of advantages. By joining the M.U.S.Z. battalions, the partisans who are part of the draft call will be under the authority of the Hungarian army of the interior. They will thereby gain relative protection against the German or the Hungarian Nazis. The M.U.S.Z. battalions are the last domain where the Hungarians can assert their national sovereignty. The Zionists can become the spoils of some kind of macabre contest:

"Let me have that Jew!"

"No, he's mine." Sometimes one has to choose between the lesser of two executioners. And succeeding in starting a rivalry between them is one step on the road to salvation. Precarious hope, but Jews cannot be too selective in their hopes for salvation.

Toward the end of April and into the month of May, many Hazalah partisans, adopting the manner, appearance, and psychology of the submissive, terrorized, and law-abiding Jew, go to the labor camps assigned them. In all the Zionist groups, the orders and directives received before departure are almost identical: among the young conscripts within the labor camps, intensify the propaganda effort for "resistance at any cost." Encourage and reinforce the liaison with the partisans previously drafted, and spread out among other conscripts. Select new activists, group leaders ready for action, from among the most resolute. Spread the word on Nazi massacres, and on the death camps. Maintain the spirit of the *Aliyah*—the "going up" to Israel. In short, prepare the youth for action. Many who have decided to avoid joining the M.U.S.Z., either by evading the draft or by getting deferred, change their minds. The rare Hungarian sympathizer encourages them in this. Such a person was the brother of the Nobel prize winner Professor Szent-Györgyi, who urged any young Jew coming to him for advice to go to the camps: "The risks will be less for you," he said. "You'll be in a group. You'll be stronger not being isolated, lost in a hostile crowd. And soon deportations will begin!"

Not all the young let themselves be convinced. Pinchas Rosenbaum, son of Kisvarda's rabbi, recalls the scene at the easy-going medical board at Kosice that examined draftees prior to induction into the M.U.S.Z.; he noticed a young Jew from Kisvarda, a recruit like himself, who was vigorously rubbing castor beans into his eyes to produce the symptoms of trachoma. Pinchas advised him to abandon the idea:

"Maybe you'll be deferred . . . but you won't be out of trouble. Come with us!"

"I'll manage better on the outside. I'll get some false papers; maybe I'll be able to cross the border. . . . You should do the same!"

Pinchas took a sheaf of Hungarian documents out of his pocket:

"Papers? There are many of us assigned to getting these into the camps. For our buddies—for you if you like! We must stay together as long as possible. Later everyone will have his mission . . ."

"No. That's too dangerous!"

Pinchas couldn't convince the boy. He was deferred and sent back home. And not long after, he was deported to Auschwitz with his family.

For the partisans who join the labor service, the important thing is to succeed in keeping the documents and introducing them into the camps. Luckily, the search by the Hungarians is cursory. Who could suspect these pale and beaten Jews with their frightened looks, lifeless as though paralyzed, made into ciphers by events? Who could imagine they would take the huge risk—punishable by death—of introducing false papers into the camp? That they would be animated by a spirit of resistance? It is well known that Jews yield under stress. They are submissive by nature, and courage is not part of their heritage. . . . Pinchas gets past the entrance guard and finds himself inside the camp, drafted, with his supply of false documents (IDs, residence certificates, Christian birth certificates, food stamps, baptismal certificates, military training certificates) and also, sewn into the lining of his pants, a metal Levente badge from the national military-training unit. The young non-Jewish Levente Hungarians wear the same caps as the M.U.S.Z. conscripts but with a badge; the badge means that a M.U.S.Z. Jew has a chance, at the right moment, to turn himself into a Levente. For Pinchas, as for many other Hazalah partisans drafted at the same time, the watchword for the days to come—and perhaps for weeks—is to work discreetly and wait.

NINE

Beams on Israel

ON ALL SIDES, the menace becomes clear. One by one the exits to freedom close: the Hungarian Jews feel the Nazi trap tighten around them, methodical, cruel, implacable, and as though reinforced by the unawareness of its future victims.

Within this system of death, hope must be kept alive by keeping not only contacts with the free world, but a concrete link, a road into the future, to Israel. It is what reason could buy. It is Operation Tijoul.

For the young Zionists, the word itself takes on, through the days and weeks, as the pace of deportations and executions accelerates, the resonance of an ultimate hope. *Tijoul*—the voyage, the escape into Israel! Even when, as often happens, the frail connections, established at the cost of great risks and terrible hardships, are broken off, the heads of Operation

Hazalah decide to maintain artificially the working of the networks. For the young, they stand for more than one aspect of the resistance plan—an ultimate recourse against the absurd, death without cause, nothingness. Many Hazalah partisans refuse by choice to set out on the routes of escape, not because of danger (which is indeed, in spite of the high percentage of betrayals and arrests, less than that one faces in Hungary itself), but because they think that by staying inside the borders they will be of more use to the future of the Zionist movement and to the realization of their dream. To know that this possibility—or at least this ultimate wager—is still available to them, even at the worst moments, is comforting. Ringed by hate, doomed to the most atrocious of deaths, fully conscious of the danger, they see shining in the night a tiny beam: Israel. And between faraway Israel, and them, a link, a word: *Tijoul.*

Keeping up the frail escape networks is therefore considered a priority from the beginning. Tijoul is the poetic, abstract element of the safeguard plan. In this improbable hypothesis, were all to fail, the networks dismantled, the bunkers discovered, the Jews come to regard the situation as hopeless, Tijoul, the last chance would remain: the possibility of a miracle. And this chance opens onto the Promised Land. It should not disappear ever, at least from the mind. And actually the roads to escape are almost always open. They are narrow, perilous, improbable paths swept by tempests of hate, cupidity, and betrayal; roads strewn with traps where many encounter torture and despair, or find death. But real connections too, thanks to which the Hazalah partisans succeed in grasping many thousands of Jewish lives from the hands of the Nazis.

When the engine of extermination starts up in Hungary, two neighboring countries offer possibilities, relatively speaking, of order and safety: Slovakia, because there the "final solution" has already been partially applied and later stopped, thanks to the intervention of Monsignor Roncalli (the future John XXIII) , nuncio to Ankara; the hunt for Jews here, for the moment, is less rigorous; and Rumania, because the current political regime is trying to free itself from the Axis and has become less a police state, more liberal.

A paradoxical situation: Hungary for more than two years has been a land of refuge for the persecuted from both of these countries; to cross the Hungarian border symbolizes salvation to them. And suddenly the land of asylum becomes a hell, and the stream changes course. The Hungarian Jews, threatened by deportation, turn toward their neighbors where terror has already struck, where the anti-Semitic fever has eased a little.

This seesaw game, dictated by the unforeseen reversal in the situation has a comic aspect that does not escape the Hungarian Jews. Even at the worst moments of anguish, humor asserts itself:

"I have only two shirts left," goes a joke making the rounds of Budapest. "How am I supposed to keep a clean shirt in reserve?"

Answer: "Wear the first until it gets dirty—then wear the second; when it's dirtier than the first, the first one will be *relatively* clean, and you can wear it and it will be fine!"

This parable points up the anguished round trip of the persecuted Jews from one side of the border to the other.

Through contacts established, by way of Turkey, with Zionist organizations in Palestine, they know that on certain nights, at secret points on the Rumanian coast, ships with no flags, their lights out, release and take on clandestine emigrants. These nightly rendezvous are rare; they can be carried out only in complete secrecy because they have to outwit the surveillance not only of the Nazis, but also that of the English, the mandate power so careful to limit clandestine immigration. This is a double resistance—the Jews have against them not only their Nazi enemies, but also the enemies of their enemies! Rarely has a cause been so isolated in a pitiless world. In Palestine itself, the Jews who try to organize these rescue operations also work in secret; the Zionists must first get past the British agents before confronting the Nazis on the coasts of Europe. But their energy never flags. Among them is a young unknown officer, Moshe Dayan, and a young man, Ben Nathan, now Israel's ambassador to Paris.

In the field, at the frontiers, the task assigned to the Hazalah agents, the Tijoul organizers, is almost superhuman. In those "off-limits" zones, as they are called, any curiosity is considered suspect. A partisan recalls:

> Every time we approached an off-limits zone, looks became more penetrating; the Hungarian police "unpeeled" our false papers. You couldn't take notes; you had to remember everything: opening and closing times at the stations, the cafés, the brasseries, the location and layout of the public parks where fugitives would eventually spend a few hours before making contact with the escape agent, or before the departure of the group, the listing of safe hotels. You had to know how to find rooms to rent in the houses of peasants, test the good will of professional smugglers, keep watch over the police, evaluate their operatives, their weapons, and if possible keep track of their routines. . . .

The police with their dogs, the gendarmes, the armed customs officers may at any moment begin to wonder about the presence of an onlooker or a stranger—even though disguised as a peasant, or going by nonchalantly with a pitchfork over his shoulder. How many Zionists have disappeared in the course of one of these reconnaissance and intelligence missions to the borders? How many, arrested and tortured, have died without talking?

As often as possible, Hazalah uses girls. A girl goes about

with an innocent, frivolous air. A couple is always less suspect than a boy or a man alone. And most of all, having no physical mark of their Judaism, women have a better chance of having their false identities accepted during interrogation.

As early as March, and in spite of the travel prohibitions weighing on the Jews, the round trips between Budapest and the Rumanian border multiply. Some partisans make several trips a week. Often they carry money to buy accomplices. In the headquarters of the different movements, intelligence is gathered; the escape strategy is beginning to take shape. The partisans' enthusiasm for Tijoul is tempered only by the useless waits, the agonizing delays. But when a partisan is arrested—which always becomes known—ten spontaneously offer themselves to serve as his relief. The hope for Tijoul multiplies their courage tenfold.

Toward Rumania, there were no networks: they had to be created. It was a difficult, exhausting, killing task. The problem was different in Slovakia, where the connections were already established; there, it was simply a matter of reversing them.

In March, in the last days of the Hungarian "independence," Jews from Slovakia, Zionist or not, fleeing the police of Hacha and Monsignor Tiso, still succeeded in crossing the Hungarian border, paying a king's ransom for complicity, dealing with escape agents on the take, or even—in rare cases—with partisans acting for the cause. The border was known to be passable even though Nazis had intercepted many fugitives. Much more information was available than about the Rumanian borders. Furthermore, the Hazalah partisans of Budapest had rather sizable amounts of Slovakian *korunas*. Slovakia was a land of partisans; Hungarian Zionists kept up contacts with Jewish resistance units who possessed networks of sympathizers, and bunkers—safe caches outside the towns, with arms. This was the main reason why Hungarian Jews preferred the Slovakian route to Israel: in Slovakia, if they were blocked, they could fight. One Tijoul connection ended in Bratislava, where Slovakian partisans maintained secret contacts with Hazalah. At first, the most-used escape route was through Kosice (Kassa). An escape agent named Duda, who until the invasion had been the contact for escape across the border into Hungary, now agreed to work in the reverse direction. Harboring the fugitives constituted the principal difficulty; the regular train coming from Budapest arrived in Kosice by night, and the problem was to lodge the Tijoul fugitives who suddenly found themselves in the streets, under the precarious protection of false identities. The difficulty increased when the Nazis chose Kosice as a concentration point for Jews in the region—because of the large brickyard that was next to the railroad. (Throughout Hungary, brickyards, always next to the railroad, served as assembly points for the victims.) The concentration brought a heavy detachment of Hungarian gendarmes into the city. The risk soon became so great that, in April, the Kosice connection had to be reduced.

The passage north through Lucenec then became the principal Tijoul road into Slovakia. A young sympathizer whose code name was Manyi had a house near the border; she herself escorted escapees to her house and at night guided them into Slovakia. Many times they were surprised by Hungarian gendarmes. By her intelligence—and also her charm—she triumphed over the most difficult situations. Many fugitives owed their lives to her.

Other connections were reversed during March. Partisans sent on missions were warned especially against agents provocateurs who swarmed across the borders. The gendarmes offered sizable rewards for all Jewish fugitives caught in the course of an escape attempt. The Hungarians thought—

wrongly—that all fugitives had "fortunes" in foreign exchange on them (actually, dollars were few, almost nonexistent in Hazalah coffers) and charged accordingly. You had to weigh any offer of help—and any mistake was paid for with your life. It was, survivors now say, a dramatic quandary: to refuse a deal because it seemed unsafe or to accept it in spite of doubts. Often, they left it up to fate. There was an agent in the Slovakia-to-Hungary route called Bela who had been very reliable; he had even provided false papers to fugitives. After the German occupation, he declared himself ready to lead Hungarian partisans into Slovakia, saying that he had opened a passage at Sassony, a place familiar to him. As a trial, a first group of three friends—three "tough guys" ready to defend themselves and wanting to join the partisans as soon as possible—was sent to him. He was trusted, though some people had reservations; but in any case he had to be tested.

The young Zionists went to the meeting. Bela awaited them. He was given the money. At the last moment, one of the partisans hesitated. To his fiancée he said, "I don't like his looks."

It became known, long after, that model escape agent Bela had warned the gendarmes. The partisans fell into an ambush in which they were outnumbered ten to one. They fought for their lives, as could be expected. No one knows the details of the fight; none of the Jews survived. But what is certain is that the traitor never reappeared. Before dying, the betrayed Zionists had time to render justice.

Treason, like death, prowled everywhere. Hillel Kohn, a Hazalah envoy, worked hard at the Slovakian border. He was one of Tijoul's most efficient relay agents. Dozens of groups had already made the transit thanks to him. He was planning to put a new connection into service, dressing the Zionists as Levente men, when he was arrested. The news was greeted emotionally in Budapest in Hazalah circles. Who had betrayed him? Had he neglected a point of security? They could only erect hypotheses; with Hillel in jail, all of Tijoul into Slovakia was threatened.

Hillel is shut up inside the Cluj brickyard with the partisans arrested with him. He knows that the future of Tijoul in this sector depends on him, and his spirit is indomitable. He communicates his ardor to the detainees: it's a duty to survive, he says. Never yield!

Almost miraculously he succeeds in convincing the Nazi who is questioning him that he is just a simple student on the run and doesn't know a thing about a would-be organization:

"I came here alone," he asserts. "They told me in Budapest that there were ways of crossing the border. But I couldn't find them . . ."

His clumsy, frightened air and imploring look convince the police that they are dealing with an idiot—one of those terrorized Jews resigned to die. So they will let him die. He is taken to one of the railroad cars being held at the brickyard.

In a classic scenario, the Jews are huddled together, the doors are padlocked, and the train moves out, toward death.

By a second miracle, Hillel has managed during the search to conceal a hatchet, lashed to the inner side of his thigh. He has had time to observe that the police only frisk the outside of the thighs. As the train pulls out, he announces his plans for escape. There are more important things to do than to die, he announces. Such is his enthusiasm that the usual obstacles (fear of reprisals, and the like) are overcome. In the middle of the night Hillel succeeds in leaving the train, after undoing a plank; a young partisan jumps with him—the minimum number thought practical in order to spare the rest of the passengers reprisals.

Hillel will join a group of Slovakian partisans; he will take part in the September 1944 insurrection. But before that he is successful in getting an essential message through to the Hazalah leaders: after intensive reflection, he has discovered the only possible source of betrayal in his network, a Hungarian railroad employee, whom he paid; from her he got information about convoys, delays, and police surveillance. An inquiry on the spot confirmed his doubts. The employee is "eliminated" by two partisans.

For the journey toward Rumania—and the distant prospect of a nighttime embarkation for the Promised Land—or toward Slovakia and its partisans, Tijoul necessarily included for the Hazalah partisans a phase of physical and psychological training. Nothing controllable was left to chance. The candidate had to change not only his identity but also his personality; to be infused with it, actually to live it, offered the only chance of overcoming any eventual police interrogation. One doesn't behave the same way, use the same words, look at things the same, move the same if you are a peasant going back to his farm, an orphan from the city joining his relatives, or a Nylas —Nazi—student obeying governmental instruction and going to work in the fields. You could also be a false agent provocateur, a false "Jew hunter" (this cover was often used), a would-be police auxiliary, or a customs officer. Or the son (or daughter) of a ranking secret-police agent, or of a commanding officer of the gendarmerie, or of a high-placed Levente instructor. In any case you were always an anti-Semite. You held Jews responsible for the war and the bombing, and you had to make this known, even to crack jokes in this direction. Never slip up, keep yourself under control, under all circumstances.

Your suitcases should never be too many, nor too big. Behavior in trains was minutely studied and rehearsed. The least error, the slightest hesitation could be fatal. Preparing for Tijoul was a strange theatrical training—but you knew what sanction awaited the bad actor: death without recourse.

The topics of conversation, as well as what tone to use, were planned in advance. The fugitive could never be too talkative—nor completely silent. He could talk sports, compare the virtues of football stars, list all the actors—the real ones—the popular ones, mention Marika Rökk's talent, and hum the songs of Zara Leander. And as they were young, the partisans had necessarily to build a Levente past for themselves, and in case they happened to come in contact with a would-be comrade, to know the names of officers, addresses—the precise details.

It was a true effort in depersonalization, all the more painful in that the trip could not be taken as a group. In this adventure, everyone was on his own in a hostile environment, isolated in a train full of enemies, a compartment full of strangers, a stranger even to himself . . . If a comrade in the train was arrested, you had to stay put. And even rejoice in the arrest out loud—this neutralization of a "Jew bastard," responsible for the war and Hungary's misfortunes.

It was a strange and heartbreaking situation. Partisans who traveled knew that Jew-hunters boarded the train with them. The smiling neighbor offering you a sandwich could very well be one of them. The curious fat woman asking questions (Where are you from? What street? What do your parents do?) might be motivated by thoughts of a reward. At the end of the journey, the unknown. In case of arrest, torture. All around them, hate and cupidity. Far behind, families, friends—with the feeling deeply planted, sharp as a claw, that you would never see them again. Some, on the Tijoul road, were not yet sixteen years old.

TEN

First Steps

FROM KOSICE, where the enrollment of Jewish recruits took place (a captain congratulated them, not without irony, for their sense of duty and patriotism), the M.U.S.Z. detachment of Pinchas Rosenbaum is moved to a small village, in the heart of the mountains. The recruits settle into uncomfortable barracks, amidst wild, impressively grand scenery. The air of the summits gives them color; under other circumstances these young men would have considered themselves fortunate in this high-altitude vacation in the beauty of the wooded slopes. But, careful to play their roles as passive and resigned Jews, the Hazalah partisans are nonetheless vigilant. On the lookout for any relaxation on the part of the cadre, they remain wary.

As soon as they are settled in the camp, brutal officers assign the conscripts to heavy outdoor work. They are ordered to fell trees, clear the hard ground over long, steep slopes—clearings that seem to have been laid out at random on the mountain. The reason for this mysterious work? The officers say they are preparing ski trails. Trails for sports, at such a time, at such a stage of the war? The absurdity of the job strikes every partisan. But perhaps the idea is a trick to test their submissiveness. They work, without objection.

Living conditions, bearable during the first days, soon worsen. Reveille is at four o'clock. The morning soup—vegetable—and the evening soup—with rare bits of stew meat—become less abundant. A new cadre imposes harsher discipline: to speak during work is prohibited; breaks are reduced.

However, an embryonic mail service operates. But it brings only bad news. Forced to undergo censorship, the conscripts have to devise a kind of code—which introduces humor into their correspondence. They write: "Here, at the camp, every day is a holiday. We eat as if it were Yom Kippur!" (Yom Kippur, the Day of Atonement, is observed by a total fast.) Or else: "We are quartered in a very comfortable fashion. You'd think you were at Succoth." (During the Succoth festival, which celebrates the exodus from Egypt, huts roofed with branches are thrown together, precarious and symbolic shelters against cold and rain.)

The partisans get news from their families in the same disguised form. From a deportation camp, on the outskirts of Lublin, a Jew has written to his parents, who forward the message to the M.U.S.Z. camp: "We never see Mr. Wiesel, and all the friends who came here before us are well lodged, as in Hsadek." The partisan who gets this note explains that Mr. Wiesel was the baker, there is no bread left—and Hsadek refers to the graveyard . . . Many boys learn through friends of the departure of their families for an unknown, but easy to guess, destination. Their morale flags; the Zionists endeavor to keep up their hope and their wish to survive in the camp.

For Pinchas Rosenbaum, religious discipline and strict

observance of ritual and the precepts of Judaism will constitute the rigid framework on which his willpower centers. This attitude will soon raise difficult problems. First, food. The dietary laws of a pious Jew, as set forth in Leviticus, are numerous and rigorous. The faithful can eat meat only if the animal has been slaughtered according to religious ordinances and completely drained of its blood. Bacon, fat, lard are forbidden. From his arrival at the camp onward, Pinchas refuses all meat, and even soup if impure bits of meat have been soaked in it. He lives on bread, ersatz coffee, and scarce lumps of sugar. His comrades try in vain to bend his determination. Occasionally, Pinchas is able to exchange his ration of soup or gruel for some marmalade or a bit of bread. . . . Very soon, several of the young Orthodox gather around him for the morning and evening prayers. A curious situation arises in the camp.

Orthodox conscripts are a laughingstock to the Hungarian cadre, but they are also subject to the disapproval of their companions in misfortune. Every level of society is represented among them: young bourgeois from residential areas as well as denizens of the underworld, hoodlums, robbers, panders. The pious young Jews, who keep the Talmudic traditions in the camp, even under the threat of deportation, at first make these people laugh—then think. Their praying, with the phylacteries strapped onto the left arm and the forehead, the refusal of nonkosher food in spite of starvation, the quiet willpower, a certain remoteness from events—all the manifestations of an unshakable Jewish faith—ultimately produce a beneficial effect. A kind of curiosity replaces hostility.

The first Sabbath is the occasion for this change in attitude. On that first Saturday, the day of rest, the sacred day devoted to the Lord and to prayer, Pinchas quietly refuses to work. The soldiers of the cadre are stupefied as they watch this conscript, immobile before his tools, despite threats and a knowledge of the cruel punishment usually meted out for insubordination. From afar, the other conscripts follow the scene anxiously. Finally, a corporal steps out of the ranks:

"Pick up those shovels! That's an order."

Pinchas makes a step forward. He is about to answer in the name of the Orthodox group; silence prevails.

"No," he says firmly. "Our religion forbids it!"

The noncom is flabbergasted. But he quickly recovers and hits the rebel with the butt of his rifle. The soldiers imitate him; with rifle butts and sticks, they rain blows on the unfortunates who try to protect themselves as well as they can. Blood spurts. Many faint and collapse. Drawn by the tumult, a lieutenant, the camp commander, appears.

"What's going on?"

The corporal explains the rebellion—and the reason for the punishment. The officer turns to the conscripts. Bloody, his face swollen, Pinchas brings himself to attention.

"Our religion, sir, forbids us to work on Saturdays. You can kill me, easily, but I won't work. You'll lose hands for nothing. Because I'll never yield."

"Sabotage!" bawls the corporal, ready to resume the pummeling. But the lieutenant gestures for him to stop. He fixes his eye on Pinchas's, and unbelievable words drop from his lips:

"You don't want to work on Saturdays? Suit yourself. Providing that in five days you do the work of six. Stand up, go and get washed. . . . Your friends too!"

Among the conscripts, total stupefaction. A practicing Jew has succeeded in obtaining what neither the "toughs" nor the submissive ones, nor any other Jewish conscript in the camp could: a breach of the regulations, a modification of the discipline! The officer has vanished. The soldiers, frustrated, assemble the men. Thereafter, derision turns into admiration. The other detainees, little by little, begin to protect the Orthodox, eventually helping them finish their jobs on Friday, protecting them against the humiliations of the cadre. The faith of the Orthodox wins them the respect of all. In the barracks, silence is kept so they can pray quietly. A nickname soon clothes all the Orthodox, in a sort of veneration both fond and respectful: they are called "God's gang."

In the camp, the letters so eagerly awaited become fewer and fewer. Then they stop completely, except those from Budapest. For the Hazalah partisans, who manage somehow to hold secret meetings from time to time, this is the sign that, in the country outside the capital, deportations have begun. The conscripts are soon to discover, with their own eyes, the appalling reality. At Kosice the Hungarian gendarmerie transfer to the SS authority the trains of deportees on their way to Auschwitz. Soldiers from the cadre, who get leaves and go to town, talk about it laughingly among themselves. The conscripts hear these accounts and clench their fists in impotence and anguish.

One day a detachment receives the order to go to town. Walking down to the valley, the youths discover their destination: Kosice's famous brickyard—where the deportees are concentrated—and their mission: to clean up.

Kosice's brickyard consists of a vast open-air courtyard and two stories of honeycomb dryers. When the conscripts enter the yard, a last Jewish family, of a dozen or so, including children, is bludgeoned into a cattle car and the sliding doors slammed shut. In a corner of the courtyard lies a huge heap of suitcases, bags, open packages, shoes, and toys, around which Hungarian gendarmes laughingly busy themselves. In the center of the courtyard are three improvised latrines, fed by two small faucets. Nearby, the kitchen: a cooking pot on a brick hearth. . . . The conscripts' mission: to clean the latrines.

"With your hands," the soldiers specify, holding their sides, "so you can find anything precious the deported have thrown there before they left. . . ."

The conscripts set to work. And, under close watch, they actually extricate a few jewels of no great value, a few coins. But the most moving finds, for the pious Jews who understand their meaning, are the wigs of married women. For fear of being selected for some military brothel, or of being coveted by the soldiers, the pious women had abandoned them there. They had tried to make themselves ugly for the trip, as a last and pitiful reflex, inherited from an ancestral habit of persecution.

In the camp, waiting becomes a form of heroism for the partisans, tense in their itch for the fight. Finally the detachment leaves that strange mountain work site. They go by foot to Hethazpuzta, then to Orkeny. At every cantonment along the way, the Hungarian soldiers conduct new searches. There are watchmen to signal the coming of the searchers. Each time, the partisans must employ infinite ingenuity to save their papers, badges, or makeshift weapons. From all kinds of clues, they realize that events are rapidly unfolding: all over Hungary deportations are being carried out. Trains have often been seen in the country, heading north. In the night, ghastly moans burst from them, and the puffing and blowing of the locomotives can't drown them out. Yet, the tactic is still to wait.

The Jewish conscripts, from camp to camp, are assigned all kinds of tasks: loading army trucks with crates of ammunition, building actual hills of sand around ammunition dumps, hauling shells and spare parts. Plans for escape, for sabotage, flash in their minds a thousand times. But always they give them up. Isn't the Hazalah watchword to melt into the mass of conscripts, never to make themselves conspicuous through any act that might reduce future chances for resistance? In Budapest, the heads of the movement are at work. They are still active, disguising Jews under false identities, looking for help from among neutral countries—an extra precaution for the time when extermination reaches its acute phase. To act precipitately and too boldly now would be to compromise the meager chances for action. True, deportations are being carried out, but unfortunately there is nothing to be done! The Jews of the provinces who gave themselves up without even attempting to escape their destiny, having neglected all advice and supplication, are condemned. To delay a train on its way to Auschwitz, to gain one day, are the chances of the Budapest Jews to be compromised?

It is a harrowing conflict that ties down the Hazalah leaders to compliance in tragedy—the deportations in the provinces—the better to fight another tragedy. All the more harrowing because nearly all the partisans have their families or relatives in brickyards, ghettos, camps, and convoys, on the threshold of death.

Around May 6, an M.U.S.Z. detachment quartered not far from Budapest walks back from work past a school where Jews of the region are assembled guarded by the police. Nearby is the railroad, where a long train of cattle cars is standing. Barbed wire has been strung around the buildings. Some of the young conscripts stop; they have recognized parents among the captives. But the police push them brutally away from the barbed wire, while the soldiers of the cadre hurry the pace. Farewells can be heard. The next day, when the detachment goes to work, the school is empty. The train has disappeared.

It is June. It is mild in the country; the sun shines, little yellow flowers grow between the railroad ties, and no one in the labor camp doubts that the final outcome is near. Pinchas has received a card—a very rare occurrence these days. A pink card, mailed from Seewald, by Schmuel, the boy who managed to be deferred because of trachoma and who had promised to send news. Seewald? Nobody ever heard of it. They won't know till later that it's the "postal" name for Auschwitz. The Nazis sometimes let messages get out.

"I arrived OK," the boy writes to Pinchas. "Your parents have already left."

The meaning of the innocuous words is clear—and at this stage of the war, considering the news that abounds in the camp, no one could mistake it. Pinchas sheds no tears. But he feels he must do something right away. If not, he'll go mad—from sorrow, impotence, impatience.

He looks at his comrades, who are watching him in silence. He sees them as he has never seen them before. And he is struck by the disastrous, catastrophic state of their clothes. They are in rags. The things wear out quickly at hard labor; without money, receiving no packages, the Jewish conscripts look like a troop of beggars. An idea occurs to Pinchas. He needs to cling to it, as small and absurd as it is, to escape despair: find some clothes for the conscripts. It is a task like any other task, tiny, immense. Like an automaton, Pinchas goes to see the officer. He waits. Then he presents his request: to go to Budapest—which is not far from the cantonment—to get decent clothes, worthy of the army, from the Jewish Central Committee.

"We are Jews, sir, but we belong all the same to the Hungarian army. In consideration of its traditions, you can't leave these men in rags. It's an insult to the Magyar military virtues that you symbolize, sir."

Once more, audacity pays off. The officer gives in. But won't the conscript take advantage of this assignment to desert? Pinchas gives his word. The word of a Jew? The lieutenant accepts it.

That very evening, flanked by a soldier of the armed cadre

(for a contradictory new regulation puts the M.U.S.Z. Jewish conscripts on the same footing as POWs), Pinchas leaves the camp for Budapest. Without knowing it, the Hungarian army aids and abets a liaison mission of Operation Hazalah.

The soldier in charge of the surveillance of the partisan doesn't know Budapest. Pinchas walks him through the noisy streets and avenues with their traffic of trolleys and a few German army cars. Many stores are closed for lack of merchandise. In the middle of the Danube, Margaret Island is still an oasis of greenery and peace. The problem is to make contact with the Hazalah people, without arousing the suspicion of the guard, who is now a little dazed. In this, Pinchas succeeds. The clothes he is there to get constitute an effective alibi. In a second-hand-clothing store, the Hazalah people bring jackets and pants and, under the pretext of wrapping packages, a secret meeting is improvised under the nose of the guard.

First Pinchas transmits all the intelligence they have gathered in the camp. He describes Kosice's brickyard; he reports on the locations of military depots; he speaks about the card he received from Auschwitz.

"We know about your parents," a leader puts in. "Cards from Auschwitz are quite numerous. They are *always* written in the first person singular, which proves that men and women are separated as soon as they arrive. There is never any mention of the children. Or of the aged. We are as deeply grieved as you are. That's why we have reserved a place for you in the next tijoul to Rumania. . . ."

To leave for Israel? Pinchas doesn't hesitate; he refuses. It's not a matter of the word given to the officer, but of the enormous job that remains to be done at the camp and in the labor service in general.

"The partisans are ready," he says. "Their spirits are excellent. They have made thousands of Hazalah adepts among the young. All are eager to fight. But they need the means to escape: false IDs, plenty of false IDs. That's the principal problem. . . ."

At the door, the guard grows impatient. "How are you coming with those packages of clothes? What's all this confabulation about?"

"Get him some wine," says Pinchas.

The time is up; the bundles are tied.

"I'll keep in touch," says Pinchas. "Prepare the IDs and a lot of them. The future of Hazalah is where we are." And he's on the road back to camp with his escort.

To keep in touch! Not long after this strange furlough the Zionists in the camp learn that all conscripts are supposed to change posts, by train this time, to Varpalota. The itinerary is through Budapest. This might be the opportunity to introduce into the camp the necessary element that has so far been missing for a massive escape—the IDs. The resistance committee assigns Josy Katz to be liaison agent. He is to escape when the convoy passes through the capital and to organize the supply of false papers. Josy is short, lively, courageous. Unobtrusive, and never having had any problem with the officers, his disappearance should go unnoticed, at least for a time. His mission is to gather as many documents as possible and to have them reach his comrades—eventually, to bring them himself. He knows camp routines and working hours. He could succeed where someone else would fail. At the same time, his job is to establish contacts with Hazalah partisans in other labor camps and to give all possible pieces of information about the Jewish conscripts to the Hazalah leaders in Budapest. . . .

Taking advantage of the slowing of the train, Josy Katz escapes. A few hours later, the regiment arrives at Varpalota, a small town 50 miles west of Budapest. Pinchas's detachment is quartered in an "evacuated" Jewish house—that is, a house whose tenants have been regrouped and deported—Rabbi Leo Singer's house. Pinchas, very moved, picks up a few souvenirs of no value, prayer books, handwritten notes, photos the looters have neglected, all that is left of a life of meditation and prayer, of a tradition carefully transmitted from generation to generation, and now doomed.

At Varpalota the work is tough, and discipline, perhaps because of several escapes like that of Josy Katz, has tightened. The conscripts are put to work breaking stones, building military roads, and making camouflage nets for airplanes. Hunger gnaws at them. Any contact with the neighboring peasants is forbidden, but some conscripts who have managed to hang onto a little money are able to get some bread. Caught doing so by a soldier one morning, a young partisan, 17 years old, is brought in front of the detachment, which is ready for work. With his arms tied behind his back, he is hung by his wrists to the branch of a tree. His feet graze the ground, and this leads him to contortions that increase the suffering even more. A sadistic new lieutenant has thought up this dreadful torture; soon, the clavicles snap, and with an agonized cry the boy faints. Brought down, doused with cold water, awakened, he is rehoisted into the same position, with his two arms dislocated. Over a two-hour period the scene is repeated three times. Motionless, the conscripts witness the torture. The watchword is not to move. But many of them swear to have their revenge one day, even at the price of their own lives. What is a human life worth in a world capable of such cruelty?

The work also consists of going to the edge of a forest to cut branches for camouflaging the planes; they have to bring back a heavy load, their stomachs empty. Some young conscripts collapse from exhaustion. Some despair. There is always a Hazalah Zionist to comfort them, to help them recover their courage; to hold on, to survive, is a duty. But will it be possible . . . ?

There is one gleam of hope in the depths of this hell. In the forest the Jews discover a kind of cabin where two spinsters live. Strangers to the world, unaware of the war and the madness of men, these creatures are followers of the Christian Sabbatarian sect (Seventh Day Adventists). Touched by the misery of the young Jews, they take it upon themselves to provide them with food. They themselves have nothing, but they have friends on the nearby farms. In the evenings, heedless of all foreseeable dangers, they prowl around the camp with bread, fruit, even milk. They refuse any payment in return; the conscripts' eyes follow their two pitiful silhouettes, silently melting into the night.

One day, they do not return. A commando unit sent to cut branches finds the poor cabin ransacked. The conscripts will keep the memory of them a long time.

Days pass, painful, monotonous. Josy Katz, the escapee, has not established the contact. A terrible doubt slips into the partisans' hearts: is Operation Hazalah suspended? Has the Budapest "center" been neutralized?

ELEVEN

Condemned Jews

TO WAIT. Not to make a move. Passive, mute, to witness from near or far the deportations, the collective murder of the defenseless provincial Jews. Such is the dreadful ordeal the Hazalah partisans endure in the early summer of 1944, hidden in Budapest, scattered in the labor camps, or on rescue missions to the borders or the provinces. To wait. Any premature act would be a desperate one, without meaning—except a symbolic one—and without result. There is still no real weakness in the Nazi apparatus, no defect that could justify a coherent action. Hungary is slowly emptied of its Jewish substance, with indifference, if not relief. Hasn't Endre, the secretary of state, declared, "Our actions against the Jews are not dictated by anybody, only by our own convictions."

The industry of death goes on unchecked; in less than two months, 140 convoys carrying 440,000 Jews are turned over to the SS by Hungarian gendarmes! It is a record; the human material to be exterminated has never been dispatched so easily to the gas chambers. During his deposition at the Nuremberg trial, Höss, commander of the Auschwitz camp, will provide tardy confirmation:

"During the spring and summer of '44," he will say with a certain pride in his voice, "we received and exterminated about 800,000 deportees from Hungary."*

One must add to this figure, for the same period, the Jews who died in the labor service and the Jews assassinated in concentration ghettos before deportation by the sinister police of Ferenczy, whose zeal sometimes went beyond the instructions regulating delivery to the Nazis (especially when a possibility of looting was in sight) . In Munkacs, for instance, as early as May, a detachment with Ferenczy himself at its head breaks loose in the ghetto. Dreadful scenes of torture take place, all for a single purpose: to get the Jews to reveal, before leaving for camp, the caches where, in the hope of returning, they might have hidden their jewels, their gold, their dollars. Of course, these caches, these fortunes, exist mainly in the feverish imagination, aroused by propaganda, of the raw policemen, most of them of peasant origin, the cockfeathers still adorning their full-dress caps! From Munkacs, however, several railroad cars filled with the pitiful belongings stolen from the Jews leave for Germany with this inscription: "Gifts of friendship from the Hungarian nation to the German victims."

In other ghettos, the gendarmerie rages with the same brutal zeal. It is not enough for the Hungarians to send the innocent to their deaths; their last moments on earth have to be made even crueler.

For the police, the problem is to keep up the "tempo," to supply the exterminator on schedule with the regulation quota of human lives. A letter, thrown no doubt from a train

* From the Nuremberg Trial Archives.

car and picked up by a peasant, described how, in June, the Jews of the Kisvarda's ghetto—that of Pinchas Rosenbaum's parents—had been regrouped:

"The community is facing considerable difficulty. The Jews are cooped up in two sawmills and in the synagogue's courtyard. The food supply is totally exhausted. Considering the great number of people and the lack of room, the sanitary situation is alarming."

The police knew how to find solutions to such problems. Veesenmayer, Himmler's emissary in Hungary, will confirm this later during his trial. His statement:

"If the Hungarians had firmly turned down the German demands, the 'solution' could not have been carried out; we had imperative need of people who knew the country, the language, the usages . . ."

During that mild summer of 1944 one train follows another, bound for Auschwitz. Only a few acts of spontaneous refusal or resistance occur. But with no organization, with no support from the population, the isolated rebels are doomed to death. At Satoraljaiyhely, a group of men who refuse to climb into cattle cars already packed with women and children is machine-gunned to the ground between the tracks. Elsewhere, young recalcitrants are tortured and killed under the eyes of the prisoners.

The Hazalah partisans grit their teeth in suppressed anger. In the labor camps they keep up their efforts at sidetracking the enemy. They are disciplined, inoffensive, submissive. Through their contacts with the Budapest organization, they know that the Hungarian Nazis are trying to unmask them and turn them over to the SS. Paradoxically, their Hungarian executioners are also sometimes their protectors; witness an exchange of correspondence between Endre's offices and the military command to which the M.U.S.Z. is attached:

"You are protecting 80,000 Jews fit for carrying arms whom the Germans are demanding from us," writes Endre.

"They are part of the Hungarian army, they are ours!" answer the military mulishly. As predicted, the conflict goes on, to the advantage of the partisans. Considering the present political confusion (Regent Horthy's actual plans are not known) and the military situation (which continues to go downhill for the Axis), their interest is in maintaining this relatively privileged situation and remaining forgotten. To wait. To be able to choose the moment to act.

Some of the young men who are more or less directly linked to Operation Hazalah are ill-resigned to this passivity. Zionist trainees, former students of community farms trained for life on the kibbutz, refugees from neighboring countries, now miraculously out of hell, are shivering with rage, with the desire for revenge and the need for justice. They are ready to place their lives on the line, to try to accomplish isolated rescue missions, even sabotage and resistance actions. They don't understand the attitude of the Hungarian Zionist leaders, their passivity, their capacity to wait, their cold-bloodedness. All they see in this posture is a kind of unawareness. Zvi Goldfarb, the Polish colossus, explains this conflict:

"The Hungarian Jews, in general, had faith in Regent Horthy. The arrival of Jewish refugees from other countries disquieted them—as if they carried about them an aura of catastrophe. In the beginning, the refugees had trouble finding rooms. Except among Zionists and some scattered elements, the atmosphere was one of optimism, confidence, immobility . . ."

Goldfarb, upon his arrival in Hungary, refuses to wait. As early as May, with his fiancée Nashka he establishes liaison with other escapees from extermination who are holed up in sub-Carpathian Russia. Soon Zvi receives a little money in Budapest and some arms for his network. At the same time, in advance of the Hazalah plan, he begins building bunkers for the final phase of the fight. During the siege his experience, his contacts, his weapons will be a precious contribution to the Hazalah youths.

Since March, Coça Grunwalt has thrown himself into an intelligence and rescue mission. Like many of the youths, he had gone to the provinces to wake up the Jews and try to save his parents. After being arrested he is miraculously released and manages to reach Vencsellö, where his parents live. Naturally no one listens to him. When the town is evacuated—all the Jews are forced to assemble in the Nyiregyhaza ghetto—he follows them. Will they understand the fate awaiting them? Coça has succeeded in getting peasant clothes for his mother, but she refuses to attempt escape.

"This regrouping won't last," she says. "Be sensible. The war is lost to the Nazis. . . . Stay with us, we'll soon return home."

Desperate, Coça destroys his own Aryan papers; he has decided to share the fate of those he has been unable to convince. He still hopes he can do something, even in the deportation train. An ordinance of the Hungarian government, summoning him to labor camp together with young men of his draft group, prevents him from carrying out his plan. He leaves the ghetto at a point when all signs indicate an imminent departure. On May 2, he is enrolled in the Kosice labor camp. And that very day, the convoy his parents are in starts out in the direction of Auschwitz.

Moshe Weiskopf also feels this cold fury and this refusal to submit to fate upon the arrival of the Germans in Budapest. He manages to get himself classified as a Hungarian Catholic, under the name of Paul Horak, printer. A quick check allows him to verify the authenticity of his papers, and he sets himself up under this new identity. With a printer friend, he begins to build a veritable reserve of Christian papers, stamps, baptismal certificates, and the like. Soon he boasts that he can turn any Jewish family into a Christian family! He has made contacts with the Hazalah leaders, but he continues to work alone. In Budapest, he accomplishes many transformations. Then the news of the deportations in the provinces reaches him. He learns that the "concentrated" Jews are then dispatched like cattle into Poland. He decides to go to the Miskolc ghetto, where his friends are. Protected by his false identity, he gets through many police checkpoints at the Budapest station. Luckily no one thinks to search the lining of his coat, which is stuffed with blank false papers and rubber stamps. At the first stop, Hatvan, 40 miles from Budapest, the train remains in the station a long time. Moshe quiets his anxiety. He learns that Miskolc is undergoing an air raid. This is catastrophic: how can he justify his presence with no luggage and no purpose for his trip? Amidst the uproar and anger, he succeeds in catching the attention of a railroad worker:

"The American gangsters are the cause of our misfortune!"

"That's true, you can say that again . . ."

Over glasses of apricot brandy, tongues loosen. Moshe—alias Horak—confides his problem to his new friend. He has to go to Miskolc; he has no money, and he doesn't know where to get a room. The railroad worker, as it happens, is from Miskolc. He offers his house. Moshe accepts.

The train leaves at night with the new friends on it, but a bad surprise awaits them: the railroad worker's house has been destroyed by a bomb.

Moshe finds himself alone again, in a strange town, with his false ID; famished, he enters a restaurant full of Hungarian officers and Nazi police off duty. Moshe wangles an invitation and, as the banquet draws warmly to a close, he joins in the vituperations against the Americans and the Jews. And he doesn't fail to add that the day's bombing has thrown him into the streets, with no hotel room . . .

Such a jolly companion is naturally invited to the officers' hotel. He shares the room of a Hungarian officer, safe from police checks or raids.

Next day, Moshe gets into the ghetto, where the Jews of the region are being regrouped. To see him arrive relatively clean and well dressed, without the Star of David, provokes astonishment. But his offers of false IDs are not well received.

"We'll be sent back home, one day soon," they say. "The police promised us!"

Unbelievable naïveté, appalling blindness. Those penned-in Jews, whom only a trip by cattle car separates from death, refuse to believe in their own ill fortune. Even though starvation, vermin, lack of water, and crowding proclaim their doom, do you treat people you intend to spare this way?

Moshe succeeds in convincing no one but the young; some of them escape and join Hazalah groups, or even the Slovakian partisans. Moshe decides to leave the ghetto; he knows that this is the turning point of his mission and that there is a good chance of his joining his fellow Jews on the train; an Aryan like Horak has no place among the Jewish refuse. Besides, what Aryan would risk mixing with them, even for the sake of some dubious deal?

With assurance, Moshe walks up to the armed guard at the gate of the ghetto. In a natural tone of voice he asks how to reach a street that he knows is very far away. By reflex, the police officer plunges into a long, involved explanation. Moshe thanks him and proceeds in the direction indicated; the officer has forgotten to ask to see his papers and query his presence in the ghetto. In the morning, the Jews Moshe left behind are herded into the cars.

While the deportations are silently being carried out in the provinces, the regrouping has begun in Budapest under the wary eye of Hazalah.

By request of the Nazis, groups of police have picked out about 2,600 houses. Big stars painted in yellow mark them for the police. Nearly 12,000 Christians live in these houses, which means little space for the "relocation" of the Budapest Jews. According to occupation authority figures, about 200,000 people, evacuated from 28,000 requisitioned apartments and residences, are to be jammed into those narrow living quarters. Such an operation seems rationally impossible. But the Hazalah observers know immediately that this inhuman plan will be carried out.

And quickly. On May 22 a Nazi inspector stops off at Budapest; he is von Thadden. He is satisfied with what he finds, since on May 26 he sends to the German minister of foreign affairs this cable: "Budapest is well in hand, surrounded by a tight belt that prevents any illegal exit of Jews."

All these moves are occasions for heartbreaking scenes; the newborn, the aged, the sick are suddenly thrown into the streets, knowing nothing of their fate. Some have time to pile their meager belongings, their furniture onto carts. Others have only suitcases. Some have nothing! Among them circulate Hazalah messengers such as Emmeric Deutsch, son of the lawyer who saved the Torahs. Their mission is to prevent panic, to reassure the most worried, to maintain calm.

"Friends are looking out for you. And will continue to do so. Don't panic, we'll keep in touch . . ."

To those who are surprised, who want to know who these Jews are who are so concerned with their fate, the partisans answer: "We are the Zionists. And remember our name—Hazalah. We shall return . . ."

In the rain, the unfortunates cross the city, hurried along by the police, rich bourgeois mixed with the little people, tailors, tanners, artisans. It is a strange exodus, a woeful procession. The Jews of Budapest are not headed toward death—not yet—but toward that half-death, an unknown house, cold, already overcrowded, where everything is lacking. Such are the apartments of the concentration, where, according to a recent ordinance, no visitors are allowed, windows are not to be opened, no one is allowed to leave even in case of air raid (but no matter, the air-raid shelters have been barred to Jews for a month).

Houses that are prisons, crueler perhaps because they do not look like prisons. Still they are overcrowded; Aryan residents, and even other Jews already more or less settled there try to protect what they have against the new arrivals. Desperate families huddle on the landings, in front of obstinately closed doors. Children squall. Women faint. The sick moan.

Outside, hurrying the bewildered herd along with their rifle butts, the police laugh or become irate, disappointed to find so little gold—contrary to what they'd been promised—no dollars and not one piece of jewelry in the suitcases they slit open, in the pockets they go through or under the skirts of the women whom they sadistically search at length on street corners.

The Hazalah partisans who have watched the concentration are unable to erase from their minds the scenes to which they have been witness. By its brutality, the transfer of the Budapest Jews foretells the next step—the deportation. Through messengers they know that convoys of the condemned are leaving regularly from Upper Hungary, from Hungarian Transylvania, from eastern regions, from the south, from the west of the country. Soon, they will leave from Budapest.

Whichever way they turn, the future is dim. To restore their courage, there is only the news from the front: in this spring of 1944, the defeat of the Nazis is certain. But for how many more weeks will the Axis hold on? Time, for the Zionists, is measured in Jewish lives. A dramatic race is under way between liberation and extermination of the last Jews in Europe. All the more dramatic for the fact that the partisans cannot yet intervene without the risk of betraying all their fragile, almost paltry provisions for resistance . . .

TWELVE

Wedding in a Cemetery

GOD HAD to be told. Not that it occurred to the pious Jews of Budapest to put on trial His wisdom, His kindness, His justice, or to entertain the least doubt about His infinite mercy. But still it seemed necessary to draw His attention to the terrifying scourge that He had allowed to fall upon His people. They had to make Him a sign.

The wise knew that under similar circumstances the just had, as ultimate recourse, launched an appeal to the Eternal; the Scriptures have preserved the record of it. A Budapest rabbi said that the example originated with the cabalist Jews of Safad, in Upper Galilee, the only town of the Promised Land where the continuity of Jewish life had not been interrupted throughout the centuries. When an epidemic of cholera developed to the point of threatening the holy and vital community in its entirety, the Safad Jews dared to appeal to God. Referring to certain passages from books, with the aid of the cabala and the example of the wise of the preceding centuries, they had found a method: they performed a wedding in a cemetery! Very near the tombs of Rabbi Joseph Karo and Rabbi Isaac Louria, the survivors of the community joined two poor young people, with all the ceremonial rites—among the dead.

God could not have failed to understand. Such a ceremony, which violated all custom and tradition, which was not blasphemous but which nevertheless skirted the strictures, was unmistakably a protest, a cry. The precepts of the religious wedding ceremony were observed, but the presence of the dead imparted a special significance: it indicated prayer, supplication, and also distress and defiance. If Almighty God could allow His people to perish from cholera, then His people could show him, with the deep respect evident in their strict observance of the laws, that they had means of expressing their astonishment, their anguish. And also that, even in their absolute submission to the Almighty, they possessed, however powerless they might be, some means of making themselves heard. Without breaking the Law in any way, without falling into sin, they—if pushed to the last resort—were able to trouble God in their turn. To press Him. The pious Jew is not without recourse in the face of divine decisions. A rabbi of Hungary confessed that he had prayed poorly on Rosh Hashanah, the day marking the new year. To one of the faithful who expressed surprise, he answered simply: "Such a year, such a prayer!" Another "hasid" had bluntly declared that he would recite only 16 of the 18 benedictions. God had to be alerted! That was the meaning of the wedding in the Safad cemetery.

The Just of the Budapest community also pointed out, parenthetically, that, afflicted by diverse scourges throughout their long and woeful history, the people of Israel had often used such means. Weddings between invalids, between paralytics, had been celebrated in other cemeteries—in Lemberg, in Krakow—to obtain the intervention of the holy souls, and finally to attract God's attention. In the face of mortal peril, the threat of annihilation, man has the right to revolt. Tradition even preserves the memory of a persecuted Jew who, before a rabbinical court, filed suit against God. He considered the sufferings he was enduring from the persecutions of the local landlord unjust and incomprehensible. For the Jewish judges, it was an unusual case. Finally, after lengthy hesitation, they accepted the suit. Legend has it that they were preparing for the trial when it was learned that the cruel lord who was the cause of this legal action, an advocate of pogroms, had been assassinated. His son, who was much more liberal, succeeded him. Of course, this had happened in the Middle Ages, not the present time. The peril had increased with time. Nevertheless, wasn't God still sole master of the situation?

Thus, in Budapest in June 1944, a strange, anachronistic ceremony took place, the response of a handful of condemned Jews, beyond the reaches of time to the Nazi threat.

It was the 33rd day after Passover, the day of Lag B'omer. In the morning, the Jews headed for the Rakoskereztur Jewish cemetery on Granat Street, in one of the city's poor suburbs, led by the community's pious rabbi, wearing the prayer shawl, the *thales*. The ceremonial canopy, the *chupa,* had been erected among the tombs by the synagogue staff, terrified by their own actions.

The bride and groom were two very young orphans; they had been told at length the meaning of this religious service, and the reason for this macabre setting. After the blessing, which froze every heart, a semblance of a nuptial banquet took place in the mortuary chamber at the cemetery gate.

Victim both of the surrounding anguish and her own disappointment, the little bride began to cry; her spouse tried to comfort her. . . . They had to go through with it. Everybody pretended to eat pieces of bread. Then Désiré Sussman, the president of Chevra Kadisha, the ritual burial society, made the speech of congratulation. Would its strange echoes find their way to God? The sad procession filed slowly out of the field of the dead, under the eyes of two old attendants . . .

By this time, most of the Hungarian Jews in the provinces had succumbed. Their deaths weighed on all the other Jews. No doubt this massacre had a meaning. Everything has a meaning where God is concerned. But excess of misfortune bears in itself a kind of nothingness:

"What could they do to you," said Abraham Ibn Ezra to a threatened Jew he was trying to comfort, "that they have not already done?"

The day takes a long time to end in the spring: the cemetery slipped into darkness. The Rakoskereztur Jews were concentrated some time later and deported to Auschwitz with their rabbi, the young couple, and the cemetery attendants. But one of them survived. If not, who would have remembered this wedding?

THIRTEEN

Fate in the Balance

THE DEPORTATIONS are interrupted! The admiral regent, under diverse international pressures, has dismissed ministers Endre and Baky, the two most efficient agents of the final solution! The Nazi agencies have left the Majestic! The police are neutralized. The surviving Hungarian Jews no longer have anything to fear.

In early July, after a period of confusion and uncertainty, of violent fighting among the shifting powers of the palace, random bits of news reach the Hazalah leaders. But they refuse to let themselves be won over to optimism. The situation of Hungarian Judaism presents a very dark picture. The name of Auschwitz is now known all over the world, as are the techniques of extermination used by the Nazis; the first statistics are beginning to be whispered—and they are terrifying.

The news about the palace is correct. For weeks the old regent of Hungary has been receiving more and more urgent inquiries about the surviving Hungarian Jews. It seems that the conscience of the world is suddenly aroused, that the scales have fallen from the eyes of the neutrals, of the high authorities.

Monsignor Angelo Rotta, nuncio of Pope Pius XII, has asked an audience of the regent and presents to him—on order of the Vatican—an open letter in which the Pope writes: "The attitude of Hungary toward the Jews is a mark of eternal shame." Gustaf V, king of Sweden, has his ambassador, Danielsson, deliver to the regent a note demanding that the deportations be stopped. Representatives to Budapest from the neutral countries—Switzerland, Spain, Portugal, San Salvador, and various South American nations—also intervene, on their own initiative or at the request of American Jewish organizations.

Obviously, the regent is less concerned with the fate of his Jewish minority than he is eager to find the diplomatic means to get out of this war already lost by the Axis; "his" surviving Jews represent—perhaps—a trump card of which he can take advantage. He decides to act. At a crown council session, he throws himself into a fit of anger, the echoes of which resound beyond the royal palace. Under its impetus, he orders his government to suspend all convoy departures. These decisions provoke a climate of violence and confusion. In the face of what they consider treason, the Hungarian Nazis hold a meeting and decide to depose the regent. They decide on a coup d'état. With Eichmann's help, and the support of the police who crowd in from the provinces under the pretext of a vague regimental celebration, Baky is to seize power; the regent and his entourage are to be neutralized.

The first measure of the new government will be to proceed with the "cleansing" of Budapest, that is, the deportation of the Jews.

Forewarned, Horthy prepares. Only one route leads to his residence in the royal palace: a tunnel whose entrance is off the cabinet room. The guard at the door is reinforced. The plot fails; the admiral regent immediately prohibits the police celebration. He orders the police to leave the city.

At various movement headquarters, Hazalah leaders keep track of the rapid developments. The tide is turning, but the game is not won. It is perhaps the calm—relatively speaking—before the storm.

On July 8, at nine in the morning, there is an air-raid alert. The non-Jewish residents of Budapest rush to the shelters. They remain there three hours, without perceiving the slightest sign of any bombing. At noon, the all-clear sounds. In regaining ground level, people discover that the police have left the city: all it took for the Baky plan to be crushed for good was for a division loyal to the regent to come forward. This easy success encourages Horthy: his vice-minister of foreign affairs goes to see Veesenmayer, the highest Nazi authority in Hungary, to inform him of the new "governmental guidelines." The discussion is fierce, but the vice minister has orders to stand firm—no matter what. Neutral protests continue to pour in, and Horthy draws encouragement from them.

For the Hazalah partisans, the regent's about-face becomes evident only the next day, July 9, when a note from the Foreign Office is sent to the representatives of neutral countries. Of course, it might be a series of traps. Or opportunistic appeasements. But at least it is the beginning of a platform, a new basis of action for the partisans. They won't fail to seize the opportunity—especially to obtain increased aid from the neutrals.

The note confirms the "temporary suspension" of convoys of Hungarian Jews abroad and authorizes a limited amount of emigration, according to the proposals of the Swedish Red Cross, the War Refugee Board, and the Jewish

Agency of Palestine. Four or five thousand Jews will be authorized to leave the country, some directly to Palestine, under the condition that they possess a certificate from the English authorities. Finally—and this point, most of all, seems rich in possibilities to the Hazalah partisans—the proposal that Jewish citizens be protected by neutral legations is accepted.

Soon Jewish leaders make contacts with neutral representatives to get protection certificates put into circulation. These certificates, duplicated by the partisans, will play an important role in the crucial moments to follow. Raoul Wallenberg, a Swedish diplomat, and Charles Lutz, the Swiss consul, are the first to receive the Hazalah representatives favorably, and to study with them ways of fighting an eventual new campaign of deportation, in the event the situation is reversed. At the same time, Jews conceive the "protected houses" scheme—in effect an extrapolation of the protection idea. A mirror company—the famous House of Glass on Vadasz Street—is officially bought by Swiss representatives from its owner Mr. Weiss, a Jew, and becomes an "annex" of the legation. Good will among the neutrals, showing itself in many places, is duly noted and carefully cultivated. But the Zionists remain very apprehensive.

Very soon, from disquieting signs, they understand that fate can be reversed, and that the threat weighing upon the Budapest Jews, though seeming to diminish, does not place them out of harm's way.

In fact, at the Majestic, Eichmann's anger has not cooled. He has communicated with Himmler and has decided to undertake a series of partial deportation operations, without any help from the police. This limits his range of action, but no matter. With the 150 German SS at his disposal, he decides to evacuate to a death camp the 1,500 detainees guarded by Hungarian police at the little Kistarcsa concentration camp.

The operation—no doubt symbolic—fails; the deportation train is stopped on Horthy's personal order! Transferred to the Hungarian police, the Jews think they are saved. But Eichmann refuses to admit defeat. Taking personal charge of the operation, he recaptures the prisoners, has them transported by truck to another station where a train is waiting. New departure. And this time, the convoy, at the speed of a main-line express, does not stop till it reaches Auschwitz. Deportees smuggled out of Hungary to feed the death mills! If the unfortunates who believed themselves saved had not thrown letters of distress through the slats of the cars, into which they had been packed even more tightly than usual, their story would never have been pieced together, and this personal action of Eichmann's would have remained a secret.

Known first to Hazalah, where the early messages arrive, then to the neutrals whose indignation redoubles (even the Red Cross interposes) , Operation Eichmann, the kidnapping of the 1,500 Jews and their illegal deportation, provokes an international scandal. But what concerns the Budapest Zionists much more than these tardy, muffled echoes of the indignation of the powers is the success of this action. It proves that the armistice between the Hungarians and the Jews is precarious, that the SS admits no defeat, and that, more than ever, it behooves Hazalah to stay on the alert, ready for the fight.

Of course, Horthy pleads ignorance. Till the end he says he knows nothing of the extermination. None of his ministers has informed him.

To a previous protest of church authorities, who show indignation that women and children are being deported along with men, hasn't the Hungarian prime minister Sztojai answered: "That is in order not to hurt the family feelings so strongly developed among the Jews"?

A Hungarian note of the same period (late June 1944)

specifies: "Hungarian Jews are not threatened by deportation. We only put Jewish manual workers at the disposal of the German government and send their wives and children with them, taking care not to separate the families. The productivity of the Jewish worker is improved thereby. . . ." (Upon arrival at camp, as we know, the women and young children are led directly to the gas chambers—as well as the aged men and the sick.)

But a very complete report, the Auschwitz log—translated by Rabbi Fabian Herschkovitz—duplicated and distributed by the partisans, has circulated in Budapest all the way up to Eichmann's desk. Thousands of leaflets have been distributed. How can the regent and his entourage truly plead ignorance with any credibility?

In May 1944 a rabbi from Bratislava manages to introduce into Hungary testimony written by two Auschwitz escapees. When they gain possession of this document—a minute description of collective assassination procedures—the Hazalah partisans decide to have it translated into several languages. But very soon they realize that the exposed facts, whose authenticity no one can doubt, are too horrible to be accepted as true by the public.

"We were in this extraordinary position," a partisan says, "of having to weaken the truth . . . in order to appear truthful . . ."

One of the first reactions of the leaders is to use this "log" to enlighten the representatives of the neutral countries, and in particular those of the Vatican. They decide that a literal Italian translation should be sent to Nuncio Rotta, dean of the diplomatic corps, bidding him to dispatch it to Rome.

A member of the religious Zionist party, Rabbi Fabian Herschkovitz, is assigned to this translation, with the aid of Léa Komoly, daughter of another Zionist leader. At the same time, a text, also under the direction of Rabbi Herschkovitz, is prepared that is more appropriate for Hungarians; oriented to their customs and their psychology, it is put in the form of a letter (the partisans have planned from the start to send it by mail to carefully chosen addresses). The nuncio receives the translated document (through the offices of a government employee, Nicolas Mester). The essentials of the pamphlet for the Hungarians follow:

TO THE HUNGARIAN CHRISTIAN COMMUNITY

In this eleventh hour of its tragic destiny, Hungarian Judaism addresses this appeal to the Hungarian Christian community with which it has shared for a millennium, within the common fatherland, the best and the worst moments. We have silently endured deprivation, the loss of our citizenship and of our dignity as human beings. We have been expelled from our homes. Now that our very existence is at stake, we launch this last appeal.

We must inform the Hungarian Christian community that, for weeks, hundreds of thousands of Hungarian Jews have been deported abroad in cruel and tragic circumstances, without precedent in the history of mankind [. . .]

Through the Jewish Council, the German and Hungarian authorities had guaranteed the security of Jewish goods and persons—on the condition that the ordinances of the New Order be respected. The Hungarian Jews have respected the laws. But the promise made them has been violated: the death trains have been dispatched from every part of the country. To this day, nearly 500,000 people have been deported. Although the ordinances referred only to regrouping the Jews, the areas set aside for these regroupings have quickly been transformed into veritable concentration camps; from there, the Jews have been sent to brickyards, flour mills, factories, etc., where living conditions are even worse. Then the Jews have been huddled into trains, 70 or 80 people to a car, under the blows of rifles, clubs, and whips. These cars, sealed, with only one outlet for ventilation, filled with humans deprived of everything, furnished only with two pails—

one of water, the other for human necessities—have ridden for days and days into foreign lands.

If the purpose of the operation had been a work camp, our anxiety would have been limited. But, without discrimination, old people, infants, the sick, pregnant women, patients snatched from operating tables were caged in these cars, and under the worst kind of brutality. One could hardly think that these people were meant to work.

According to an article published in the May 23 issue of *New Generation,* in one convoy, leaving from Nagyhazpuzta, three women were dead upon arrival at the Szombathely station. One was 104 years old, another 102, and one 92 years old. The 102-year-old woman succumbed from pneumonia. It is hardly plausible that she had been deported as a worker. Like the other Jews, she was doomed to extermination.

The experience proves that such facts are unknown to the Hungarian public. The press breathes not a word of it. Will the Christian community remain unmoved? [. . .]

Is it normal, is it justifiable before history that six out of 100 Hungarian citizens—almost a million souls—could be condemned to annihilation without having been sentenced by a court, without having had any right to speak?

We are defenseless. However, we stand up, our heads high. If we are guilty, our guilt comes out of the system that has been dominant in Hungary and throughout the world for a century; everyone is guilty with us. [. . .] Beyond political conflicts, there is a human—eternal—justice. Those who transgress it will be guilty before God and before history.

At this time of ultimate peril, let us remind you that in 1941, during the census, and at a time already critical for the persecuted Jews, they asserted, by a vast majority, not only their Hungarian language, but their Hungarian nationality.

The Hungarian nation has the right to reject its Judaism. But for that, will it sentence women, children, severe war casualties, without weapons and without defense, to a pitiless death? Would that not be in violation of all the nation's tradition of honor?

We ask the Christian community to make it possible for the

nearly 100,000 surviving Hungarian Jews to emigrate. We ask it to make contact with neutral nations likely to facilitate this emigration. [. . .]

In the name of our children, our aged, our wives, in the name of all of us, doomed to near extermination, we address a last appeal to the Hungarian Christian community. We keep our faith in its sense of justice, which cannot allow this massacre of innocents to be carried to completion.

If this last plea is denied, we ask the Hungarian nation to spare us the tortures of deportation and to exterminate us at home, on our native soil.

The arguments and style of this pamphlet might give us pause today. Yet in fact it is a model of reflection and intelligence. Every clause had been carefully weighed and discussed, every sentence analyzed for the association of ideas it could awaken in the mind of a Catholic reader. To judge this text, one must put oneself back into the actual context of the time and know fully the traditional Hungarian mentality. The partisans had to avoid the pitfalls of making charges, of being defensive, of alleged revelations—at a time when propaganda was rampant. At the same time they had to be careful not to offend the Hungarian government, to alienate the neutral; they had to take account of certain extreme attitudes of the time. It was a delicate, difficult job, to which Rabbi Herschkovitz, helped by the partisans, devoted all his care and his skill with language.

While the Auschwitz log was addressed to all the neutrals in Budapest and circulated in intellectual circles—or what was left of them—the pamphlet, run off on the duplicating machine in the Jewish Orthodox "soup kitchen," was mailed in all kinds of envelopes by Hazalah messengers. Mailing lists had been established; several thousand pamphlets were sent out during June. Very rapidly the Hungarian police, the government, and the agencies at the Majestic found out about the operation. Krumey, Eichmann's assistant, flew into a rage; he issued an order to arrest at any cost the instigator of the operation—obviously one of those "Zionist bandits." And to question him in such a way that he would expose his accomplices.

Having learned of the police inquiry, the Zionists redoubled their caution in reproducing the pamphlets, sending out letters, and buying stamps. "Operation Information," for a time, took priority in the Hazalah program. Particularly because its effects were being felt; some recipients were turning into precious (and benevolent) allies. Anonymous letters of support arrived, also by mail, at the Jewish houses. Jews received, furtively, by night, food, packages of medicine, and even money.

But the police did succeed in obtaining one piece of information. The Grunwald brothers, two young professors, were turned in and arrested in the act of distributing the pamphlet; a teacher, Denis Laczer, followed.

They underwent all the refinements of Gestapo torture for several weeks—but did not talk. We know little of how they died. In any case, to shorten their suffering, the movement got a message through to them: "You can talk." They gave some names—Rabbi Fabian Herschkovitz and Rabbi Nicolas Pehner, who they believed had left Hungary (as was rumored at the time of the arrest). But their departure had been postponed, which the unfortunates did not know. The two denounced men were arrested. Rabbi Herschkovitz recalls:

> I was in one of the "protected houses," at 29 Vadasz Street. Two inspectors showed up. They asked me to come out—if not, my parents, who were under Swiss protection, would be arrested. I obeyed, and immediately I was submitted to a flood of questions: "We know you are the author of the letter to the Christian community, and author of the translation of the Auschwitz log. We want to know who gave you this report. Who? How? We know how to make you talk. . . ."

Fabian Herschkovitz was thrown into a cell of the political prison, in the former youth house of the Hungarian steel-workers' union. Through the window, he could see the shower installations of the place, and he expected to be gassed—in accordance with what he had read in the log.

He was not gassed, but subjected to torture, day after day. Gestapo and Hungarian police took turns. The prisoner knew that, outside, the partisans were attempting the impossible to save him, and this thought sustained him. He asserted that the original text had been given him by a certain Mayer, whom he knew—without any doubt this time—had since left for Switzerland. He managed to stick to this version till August 20, the date on which the new "liberal" government led by Lakatos was put in office by the regent. After that, his tortures ceased and the accusation of treason was replaced by one of infraction of the press laws. Gasping with exhaustion, Fabian Herschkovitz was transferred to the precinct, then released. His companion, Rabbi Pehner, who had also resisted torture, met his death later via deportation.

Among the more liberal measures enacted by the regent, the half hopes of possible emigration especially interested the Hazalah partisans. Would it really be possible to send Jews from occupied Hungary to Israel? To have an official—legal—Tijoul doubling the escape networks at the borders? Immediately, talks began with the neutral consulates who had contact with England, the mandate power. This started the hunt for "visas"—which was to become one of Hazalah's concerns, along with the search for a neutral passport of convenience, then for the certificate of protection—the famous *Schutzpass*.

Clearly, the occupying Nazis were going to put obstacles in the way of these (still theoretical) departures. The action of "contraband" deportation achieved by Eichmann proved that they were not disposed to give up their prey. And from certain signs the partisans felt that the Germans were hardening their position. The Nazis, we know now, had decided to resume the deportations as soon as possible and in the intervening period to put a stop to all Jewish emigration, in spite of their apparent indifference to it. Behind this intransigence stood one man: Mohamed Amin al Husseini from Berlin, grand mufti of Jerusalem. He conducted a loud campaign of hate. Following are excerpts from a letter he sent on June 22, from Berlin, to the Hungarian minister of foreign affairs in Budapest:

Excellency:

This war has seen many Balkan Jews emigrate to Palestine. The bimonthly Jewish *Palestine Newsletter,* in its issue of May 5, 1944 (number 157) writes: "In April, 1,000 Jews arrived from Europe." The German newspaper *News from Arab Countries* reports that Jews frequently arrive in Palestine through Turkey. In the London *Times* (March 24, 1944), one reads: "Since the beginning of the war, the *Aliyah* movement alone has succeeded in entering 5,000 child and adolescent Jews from the Balkans into Palestine, thus snatching them from Nazi atrocities. Many among them, once their health has been restored, join the Haganah. Others receive farming or craft educations." This is only one feeble example of the damage that the emigrant Jews—whom I had already drawn to the attention of the Hungarian government—can cause. I also want to point out to Your Excellency that the emigrant Jews are likely to take with them secrets, and then make the most of their hidden connections. And that their arrival strongly displeases the Arabs, who are surprised to see these people coming from friendly countries.

While affirming my admiration for the Hungarian anti-Jew laws, I ask of your Hungarian government to do what it can to prevent the Jews from going, legally or clandestinely, to Palestine, by way of Rumania, Bulgaria, or Turkey—in the interest of the Hungarians and of the Arabs. . . .

Signed by the hand of Mohamed Amin al Husseini, grand mufti of Jerusalem.

Who, some years later, in Palestine, will preach the Holy War against those rescued from Auschwitz.

During his trial, Eichmann contended he had never had any contact with the grand mufti of Jerusalem:

"I never saw him," he declared. "I know nothing about him. I didn't even know of his presence in Berlin."

A few days later, the same magistrate asked him a question concerning a Jewish leader of Budapest, Philippe Freudiger.

"Did you know him?"

Eichmann reflected.

"Freudiger . . . Freudiger . . . Of course, yes. He wore a beard . . . exactly like the grand mufti of Jerusalem."

FOURTEEN

The Closing of the Borders

IN BUDAPEST, crossroads of contradictory rumors and false reports, moments of hope and confidence alternate with periods of depression. Like all the surviving Jews, the Hazalah partisans are subject to this ebb and flow. But their work is not affected.

Tijoul, for instance, goes on, despite the possibilities of legal emigration that new provisions of the government seem to open—rather obscurely to be sure.

Volunteers to organize Tijoul, to keep check on the connections, to maintain contacts despite the enormous risks are never lacking. All want to work for the escape. Very few accept escape for themselves.

This is truly the expression and fulfillment of the partisan spirit. One of the most intrepid of those involved on the

Rumanian border is Moshe Pil (Moshe the Elephant). His headquarters are located at Nagyvarad. He is usually accompanied on his assignments by a Jewish girl called Anna. Both of them often assume new personalities and identities. Their adventures are legendary.

One day, disguised as a farm worker, Pil heads for the border with Anna. A farmer, a fellow traveler (and venal too) serves as escape agent for the fugitives. The partisans arrive in a horse-drawn wagon and are greeted by the peasant's wife, in tears; her husband has been arrested that very morning by the Gestapo.

Pil thinks quickly. He hasn't spotted anything, but he is certain that the farm is ringed by the police. He has fallen into a trap. His one small chance is to make a rapid move that will surprise his opponents.

Pulling Anna along with him, he jumps into the wagon and whips the horse. But hardly has the wagon gone five yards when a man leaps onto it and sits beside the two Jews on the driver's seat. Obviously a policeman. Pil and Anna pretend to be surprised; what does he want from two harmless peasants like them? The man doesn't answer. Thinking very hard and watching for a chance to run away, Pil and Anna keep up a cheerful chatter in the regional accent, like the two careless sweethearts they are supposed to be.

The wagon comes to a bridge. A child, four or five years old, frightened by the noise, steps to the side and falls into the river. Reflexively, Pil leaps up. He dives, reaches the drowning child and hauls him, choking and muddy, up to the bank. The parents are there, quite hysterical. When Pil, dripping wet, gets back to the bridge, the policeman is standing by the side of the wagon. Pil thinks he sees the hint of a smile on his face. Anna, on the seat, doesn't make a move. Finally, without a word, the policeman goes back by foot to the farmer's house. Is he giving the two Zionists a present—

their lives? They don't dwell on it; right then there is only one concern: to find shelter, to preserve their miraculously spared freedom. The policeman might change his mind and come back. They still have many people to save. The next day they are in Budapest.

A short time later, they put the finishing touch to what will be known among the Hazalah youth as the sleeping-car Tijoul! Since the train from Budapest arrives by night at Nagyvarad, there is a serious problem of lodging for those who intend to cross the border. The hotels are under surveillance. Where to put the fugitives? Pil suggests that they travel by Pullman; he has noticed that surveillance is less strict at arrival checkpoints. The Hungarian police are unable to imagine that a fugitive would be bold enough to mix with high officials, diplomats, officers—the normal and logical users of the first-class accommodations. There are other advantages to the scheme: it reduces the risks of denunciation, and it enables the fugitives to leave their compartments rested and washed in the morning. It is blending with the enemy, the better to mislead him. But it also requires nerves of steel, and behavior adapted to the situation.

Several groups have no trouble getting to the border this way. Then—predictably—something happens. Pil himself, inventor of the scheme, is its victim. He is traveling by sleeping-car under the alias of a Hungarian secret-police agent and is in charge of escorting six escapees scattered here and there in the train. Soon after the departure, at Szolnok, he finds that the Hungarian police have spotted one of the Jews—traveling third class. He strongly hopes, he wants to believe that this arrest is a mere accident. It has happened before that a soldier or a passenger recognizes and denounces a Jew. But at the next station Pil sees on the platform three other fugitives in the custody of the police. Beyond any doubt the police are acting on some information. One more "friend" is left on the train. Pil sees him coming down the car corridor between a plain-clothes inspector and a policeman. Pil is standing in the door of his compartment, but he can't make a move without being suspected. Besides, he is afraid that the young man under arrest will by some gesture or even a look draw the attention of the police to him. The group stops a little way off. If the captive has seen Pil, he has not let it show. As the train heads for the border, Pil is obliged to listen to an inspector bragging on and on about the arrest on the train of four Jews who were captured, false IDs and all. The fifth has yet to confess he's a Jew. But it won't take long. . . .

Under Pil's eyes, almost within the reach of his hand, the police tie the young man by the wrists to the luggage rack of a compartment. They take off his pants. And as the young man persists in his denials, maintaining that some unlikely surgery had been performed, they begin to torture him. Drawn by the noise, the passengers—all dignitaries of the regime—crowd against the compartment door. At that time, in Hungary, the sight of a Jew being beaten by the police is no rare thing. But the singular setting, the nakedness of the young man hanging by his wrists, the ardor of the policeman beating him with his leather belt, add sadistic spice to the monotony of the trip. Soon, over the moans of the victim, the spectators' voices keep time with the blows, chanting "Yid! Yid!" Bets are made: he'll confess—he won't! They egg on the policeman who relieves the inspector.

"My blood was boiling," Pil recalls. "Even today—after 25 years—I wonder how I was able to control myself. Finally, the poor young man fainted. But his heroism was not for nothing. Exhausted—and proud of their prowess—the police neglected to check the other passengers in the sleeping car. My papers were impeccable, but that day, surely, I'd have been betrayed by the way my hands quivered with anger."

Pil the Elephant becomes a figure almost legendary among

the Hazalah partisans in hiding in Budapest or in the M.U.S.Z. labor camps. A hundred stories of audacity and heroism are told about him.

Another character, Uncle Peter, an escape agent, also provides material for many a conversation:

An old Hungarian peasant, he is a follower of the Sabbatarian sect who considers it an overriding duty of charity to help the persecuted Jews. The messengers to the borders discover him and use him as a relay; he refuses any payment. He gathers the fugitives into shelters in the woods; all night long they talk about religion and philosophy. The Zionists he guides to Rumania embrace him and later, if their trips end well, write him in homage.

When it comes time to leave a group in the dark of a moonless night, Uncle Peter always kneels and says a prayer. With simplicity, he declares that the purity of his heart is the warrant of his prayer's effectiveness. He has infinite confidence in the goodness of God.

The partisans also discover that he has a gift for organization—a rare and looked-for virtue among the friends of Tijoul! Uncle Peter is ultimately put in charge of a real staff. He works hard. He saves many lives.

He succeeds in avoiding all the traps set by the Gestapo and carries on his job until the liberation. Then he returns to his prayers.

Unfortunately, the Hazalah partisans had only one Uncle Peter in their service, and in most cases they had to deal with paid escape agents. Paid, and therefore easily lured away, not above the double cross and blackmail. Against such eventualities, the partisans were almost helpless. Their only defense was their vigilance, an ever-present awareness of danger, and quick reflexes.

Some never came back from the borders. Betrayed, arrested, deported, or shot on the spot. Often tortured. But they didn't talk.

Some failed, survived, and returned to Budapest to try again, so relentless were they in their flight from the specter of deportation; so determined to survive.

Imre Hertz, called Mimish, had organized the production of false papers on a large scale in Budapest. Denounced, spotted, trapped, he decided to take his chances getting to Rumania. A first try failed; the escape agent had disappeared. But the applicants finally managed to get back to Budapest. A new "convoy" was prepared, which had to go through Szeged, Hungary's second city, in the southeastern part of the country. Mimish got himself into the group along with Juci, his wife.

No sooner does the train start than alarming signs appear; one of the passengers, in second class, is obviously an informer looking for information. To disarm him, one of the undercover Jews declares himself a police official. The informer retreats. After many lengthy and minute checks, the group finally reaches its destination. Later, on a moonless night, the thirteen escapees, led by an agent, silently proceed toward the border.

Suddenly, at a curve in the path winding through firs, emerge menacing shadows; they hear the much feared guttural "Halt," the rattling of guns being cocked. In such situations, the partisans' watchword is, "Every man for himself." It is a scene the Hazalah specialists have made them study and rehearse carefully many times. Mimish rushes into desperate flight, at right angles to the planned route. Juci runs in another direction. But in their separate flights, she is stopped by a new barrage, and so is he. There can be no doubt. It is an ambush. The 13 have been betrayed.

Any resistance is unthinkable; the fugitives give themselves up. Their hands tied behind their backs, they are driven through the night under the bludgeoning of rifle butts to the Szeged prison. Mimish has abandoned all hope. Juci and he will have failed in their Tijoul! Rare are the partisans arrested at the border who emerge from the police jails alive. In the Gestapo car, the two young people exchange a last kiss and a pledge of love.

A week later the "escape agent" presents himself to the Hazalah leaders in Budapest, asking for what they owe him. However, one detail alerts the partisans: the man cannot produce the letter from Mimish which should serve as proof. He claims he was arrested by the police on his way back and was forced to tear up the letter. Prodded with questions (according to a well-tested method), he gets tangled up in his answers. Finally, the leaders are certain that the man is lying and that, consequently, Mimish's group failed to get through the snares of the net. The "agent" is put on the blacklist, and an investigation begins. It takes ten days to reach some conclusions. And what the Zionists discover astounds them.

Mimish, his wife, and Hans, another partisan, have escaped. Taking advantage of the dark and of a single moment of inattention on the part of the gendarmes, they manage to jump out of the Gestapo car in the outskirts of Szeged. Without identification, without money, their chances of remaining free are almost nil, but they happen to run into a road-repair crew of Jewish M.U.S.Z. conscripts. Among the workers are some Hazalah boys. A brief conversation, and the fugitives receive slices of bread, a little money, and a precious piece of information about the only possible hideout around.

"Thank you, *shalom*. . . ."

But a Hungarian soldier looms up. Those three strangers with their torn clothes, their faces furrowed by exhaustion, puzzle him. He calls for help, while menacing them with his weapon. Again, they have to flee. The three partisans scatter; but this time, only Mimish manages to vanish into the forest. Bullets whiz past his ears. Juci and Hans are arrested once again.

When he finally reaches Hazalah headquarters in Budapest, Mimish, famished and sick, does not know what has become of his wife and Hans. Perhaps they have been wounded by the soldiers' bullets, or put to death in prison. His friends—Efra in particular—do their best to soothe him.

The partisans' efforts to get more news are in vain. Mimish is desperate. Adding to his anguish is the feeling that he has abandoned his wife to the enemy. He spends hours without speaking, without moving, staring vacantly into space. He is unable to sleep.

The partisans take great care to keep up morale among themselves. It is the only effective weapon the organization possesses in abundance, a psychological weapon, but a powerful one. In no time, everybody knows the story of Juci's arrest—and of Mimish's despair. Something must be done. But all attempts at getting information fail. Silence settles on the group.

When all the sources seem to have dried up, miraculously, some news comes in. A Serbian member of the Gestapo, called Milan, presents himself to Rafi, one of the Hazalah organizers. He bears a brief message from Juci:

"Being tortured. Can't hold out much longer. Trust Milan."

The policeman reveals that the group is being held in Bacstapolya, a German camp known to Hazalah, near Szeged. They are all alive but regularly submitted to cross-examination by investigators brought from Germany. Especially Juci: the Nazis have established that she is the wife of the Hazalah specialist in false IDs, and they have decided to get the maximum of information from her.

"How?"

Milan refuses to answer. But his silence speaks volumes. Juci has begged him to tell the partisans in Budapest. He has agreed. Why? Because. Without trying to understand, they have to trust him. Besides, as he makes clear, they have no other choice. And they must act quickly.

Mimish knows Milan: he had met him once in Budapest, at the Gestapo, during an identification check. The policeman gave him a cigarette. As the questioning was resumed in jail (Mimish, finally, was freed, which indicates the quality of the false documents he made), Milan lent him his razor. But remembering all this does not clear up Milan's motivations: lure of a profit, guilt feelings, hatred of the Croatian Nazis? This man is a disturbing case. But—as he says himself—they have no alternative but to trust him.

Milan declares he is ready to leave for Bacstapolya to try to free Juci. His conditions are simple: he wants to be accompanied by another young woman. Why? That is his plan, and he refuses to elaborate. The partisans are in a quandary. Finally, they agree.

A much-trusted girl is assigned to this special mission: Zipi, 18 years old, small and frail, but with boundless energy. She is engaged to a Hazalah pioneer, Efra (everybody knows of their love), but they are both ready for any dangerous mission. She carries poison with her in case the whole operation proves a crude trap, as many fear. And she also takes some with her for Juci, her comrade.

On their way, Milan tells her what he has seen in the prison: Juci was subjected to a "special treatment." The Nazi police, sadistic and imaginative Germans and Hungarians, decided to make her into a mop, a household utensil. She is a proud girl. They forced her to roll naked on the floor, flooded with water, or on the concrete pavement of the courtyard. When she weakened, they kicked and pushed her along with their boots and riding crops. Bloody and naked, her body sore, she was "stored" for the night, with the brooms and the garbage, in a kind of closet, very cold and swarming with rats. She was going mad, but she didn't talk. Milan had been touched by her pleas.

Zipi listens and nods. She is under orders to "play" total credulity and confidence. Only later does she learn that Milan has not invented any of it. And she enters the German camp at Bacstapolya.

Milan has worked out a plan; to his chief, a Hungarian senior officer, he introduces Zipi as his sister-in-law.

"She's the one who takes care of my place, since my wife got sick," he adds. "But she needs some help. Would you please, sir, let me choose a maid from among the female prisoners?"

To select his "help," Milan goes to the prison at a time when only low-ranking guards are there. Specialists would not have released Juci to him. And not long afterward, Milan brings Zipi and Juci to Budapest. The success of this daring rescue restores confidence to the Zionists. Milan becomes one of Hazalah's surest cards on the Rumanian border. He manages to bribe several guards at the Bacstapolya camp, and he frees the other captives from Mimish's group. His activities spread to other border camps, where rescues as difficult are just as successful.

Who is this Milan? The Hazalah partisans are forever unable to pierce the mystery. He is indeed a member of the Gestapo, but also a patriot Serb. He never hesitates to risk his life to save Zionists. He accepts only the minimum pay. He speaks very little. He becomes another of the popular figures among the partisans.

One day, he fails to return from a rescue mission. Soon it

is learned that he has been arrested by his own comrades. Of course he denies all the charges against him. Using the network he has created inside the police, the partisans get him out of jail. Once free, he lets his beard grow, has a false ID made for him, and plunges into the underground for good—like any other partisan. And he continues to prepare Tijouls.

August 23, 1944, Rumania changes sides; its troops rally to the Red Army, whose irresistible advance has reached the foothills of the Carpathians. The border between Rumania and Hungary is immediately declared a combat zone and is occupied by elite German troops. Hazalah escape connections are thereby neutralized. It is the end of the Tijoul to Rumania. But, as the grand mufti proclaimed—several thousand Jews have succeeded in reaching Palestine. There, like the Hungarian Zionists, they prepare for the fight.

FIFTEEN

Sabotage

AUGUST 1944: the Reich is nothing but a besieged fortress, with wider and wider breaches, ever more numerous. After Rumania, Finland chooses a new chief of state, the independent Mannerheim. The Allied troops approach Paris. Regent Horthy knows which way the wind blows and where his last chance lies. He is afraid that Rumania's about-face will cost his country Transylvania, where he was born—it is his greatest fear. He is ready to negotiate, to play his last trump card: the surviving Hungarian Jews, whose lives hang by a thread.

He discharges Stojay, the prime minister who has been at Berlin's beck and call. His next move is to dissolve the parties, then to appoint a new head of government, General Lakatos, who is invested by the same deputies who had invested his

Nazi predecessor. It is a subtle move; Lakatos should be reassuring to the Germans, and he is not a politician. In his first radio address, on August 20, Lakatos speaks harshly of the Jews—but he announces, among other decisions, that their fate from now on falls within the sole jurisdiction of his government.

The Zionists take careful note of this statement. But they are cautious, awaiting concrete developments.

The first events are rather reassuring: Zionists in observation posts, in various internment camps around Budapest, confirm the release of Jewish captives. But a countermeasure follows immediately: some released Jews are arrested again. Five regrouping camps have been created around the city. Horthy is said to have been forced by Veesenmayer to make this decision. Finally, the regent has yielded to the Nazi representative, but the measure will not be carried out. Horthy, rid of Baky and Endre, plays to the hilt his Jewish card, a token of resistance to the defeated Nazis. The partisans wonder how far he'll go along this difficult diplomatic road, how far the Germans will let him go.

On the 24th, an ambiguous new measure lending itself to various interpretations is issued: all Jews (men and women), from 14 to 70 years old, must appear before the draft authorities to see who will take part in "military-installation work." According to the ordinance, Jews declared unfit will be regrouped in camps 30 miles from Budapest, under International Red Cross supervision.

The way of salvation? A trap? The partisans look for an answer. For the able-bodied, the new arrangements change things very little. Thirty draft groups, from 18 to 48 years old, are already enrolled in the M.U.S.Z. But what about the younger ones? The women? The infirm?

This measure, too, will not be carried out. Moshe Krausz, director of the Palestine office in Budapest, who—parallel to the Hazalah youth—wages an ardent and courageous fight against the Nazis, makes contact with the representative of the Hungarian Red Cross. He succeeds in proving to him that the camps chosen offer none of the lodging and health conditions required.

During these days of relative peace, the partisans relax none of their efforts.

"What matters is not so much what the Hungarians are doing," one hears on Laudon Street and at other Hazalah locals, "but what the Germans are up to."

A wise analysis. Eichmann has left Budapest with his staff, but he has promised to return very soon. Actually, he is "somewhere in Hungary," with Baky and other Hungarian Nazis; Himmler has advised him to "take a vacation" and await his hour, meaning the hour for deporting the last Hungarian Jews!

Nevertheless, Horthy and Lakatos execute their plan of "winning back" national sovereignty. Abandoning actions against the Jews is part of the plan, the goal of which is to make possible, at the best moment, the reversal of alliances, following the example of Italy or Rumania. An objective observer of that period could not help but be struck by the unrealistic nature of the policy. Even in protecting his last Jews, can Horthy really think that, in the light of his past, he can turn himself into a democrat, not to say a "Resistance" fighter, and take his place at the side of the Allied chiefs? In any case, he acts accordingly, and the country plays his game. As for the Jews, they sigh with relief. Their hope is fed, among other things, by all the rumors that are circulating in Budapest: secret negotiations with the Allies are going forward, as is the cease-fire with Russia; an armistice is in sight. No matter how, the end of the war is near. Paris has just been liberated; German cities are leveled by the bombings. Hitler himself thinks of suicide. . . . After all the anguish, it is an easing of the tension. But not for the partisans.

In the houses of Budapest, stamped with yellow stars, in

the labor service, wherever the outcasts lie in wait or hide, they stiffen their determination. They refuse to lose themselves to this new intoxication; almost certain that the last sorely awaited minutes will be preceded by a quarter hour of terror, they speed up the establishment of their defense network, the messenger system, the bunkers. Through Moshe Krausz, they pursue their talks with the neutrals who might provide protection or approve emigration; meanwhile they gather weapons.

More than to the vague rumors of armistice, cease-fire, or peace, they listen to the echo of the violent combats the partisans have just begun in Slovakia. Hitler himself, it is known in Budapest, accuses the Jews of having originated the insurrection. This accusation fills the Zionists with pride, though it is, in many regards, exaggerated: very few Jews remain in Slovakia at this time; the survivors take part in the fighting with ardor and enthusiasm, but all the credit can not be given to them. Among these fighters are many partisans from Budapest who have followed the Tijoul road since March 19.

Hazalah watches their fight with passionate interest; at last, organized Jews, disciplined, well armed, are fighting openly against the Nazi enemy! Partisans dispatched to Banska-Bistrica, in Slovakia, the headquarters of "Free Czechoslovakia," return to Budapest with comforting news: Jews are in uniform! Among them are kibbutz *halutzim*—partisans from Palestine—parachuted into the theater of operations. Thus is accomplished the junction of the Zionists of Europe and the Jews from the Promised Land. The toughest fighting takes place in the mountains. At their own request the Jewish partisans in Slovakia and the Hungarian escapees are scattered among all the units, not formed into an independent Jewish unit. This precaution is dictated by a painful experience in Yugoslavia: formed as a Jewish brigade, Yugoslav camp escapees had been engaged the year before, as their baptism of fire, against "Panzerdivision Prinz Eugen," the best German unit operating in the Balkans. Strategic error? Ignorance? A deliberate—or unconscious—will of the command to eliminate Jewish combatants? Whatever the intention behind the operation, the combatants of the Jewish brigade, physically weak, hastily trained, ill equipped, were wiped out in that hopeless confrontation, as surely as in the death camps from which they had escaped. . . . So warned, the Slovakian Jews ask that they be placed, without discrimination, among the combat units. Thus they feel protected from their friends!

It is even said that Slovakian Jewish partisans have taken German prisoners.

In Hungary, many partisans, simmering with impatience, wonder if the war will end too soon for them to be able to avenge their dead, to stand up to the enemy. In the labor camps, they await orders to rally to Budapest. For the sake of morale, to show that the moment for revenge draws near, Hazalah leaders decide to launch, or to pave the way for, several isolated actions.

At the Franz Josef Station, the M.U.S.Z. unit Emmeric Deutsch belongs to is assigned to unload coal. The partisans see the possibility of mixing stones with the coal. Somewhere, jammed locomotive boilers will explode. A freight train or a deportation convoy will perhaps be stopped for a while. On the approval of their leaders, the percentage of stones increases. What the partisans don't know is that the Gestapo has been alerted and is already looking into the sabotage. And the day arrives when all Deutsch's company is assembled at dawn near the Franz Josef Station. A German noncom reads a brief note: "The Gestapo, having discovered which unit of the M.U.S.Z. is responsible for sabotage against the Reich, orders that it be decimated on the spot. One Jew in ten will be shot immediately." The cadre sergeants begin at once to count them off.

Deutsch closes his eyes. He is the ninth. He sees his best friend—a partisan too—heading for the wall, with a sad little smile. . . . The rat-a-tat of firing, echoing through the empty sheds, seems to go on forever. So many Jewish partisans killed for a few hours' delay of a train, for a jammed boiler. . . .

The next day, having noticed that the number of workers assigned to the train cars changes every day, Emmeric Deutsch hides in an empty car, and when night falls, he escapes. He wants to avenge his comrades. But first he must retrieve his soul. He prays all night. "God resides where all else is forgotten."

Will the truce last? In the first fogs of the waning summer, hope fades as the days shorten. In the West, the Allied armies slow their advance. The Soviet soldiers are quartered in northern Hungary. Time passes, and the fate of the Hungarian Jews is not yet settled.

At Hazalah they ask themselves questions. From all sides come messages of impatience and anxiety: the partisans are being strangled by inaction and doubt. Meanwhile, some work is done in Budapest. "Neutral" friends such as Raoul Wallenberg, Swedish ambassador, or Consul Charles Lutz of the Swiss embassy are ready to intervene. Already numerous passports have been distributed to Jewish families, so many that von Thadden, the vigilant Nazi inspector, has become concerned. In a telegram (NG 2260 C XXIV) addressed to Berlin, he suggests advancing the date of the action in Budapest.

These neutral friends have already shown the extent of their commitment: Wallenberg went in person to pick up Jews "under Swedish protection" whom the Germans had scheduled for "contraband" deportation from the Josefvaros substation.

Charles Lutz, working with Krausz, turns the House of Glass on Vadasz Street into a refuge flying the white-cross flag. Every day lines of Jews form at its door in hope of receiving protection papers. Almost everyone gets one, because the Hazalah partisans have developed a certificate-duplicating system that—under Elisabeth Eppler's driving force—is working at full capacity.

To the partisans who try to analyze the situation, the truce cannot last long. Nazism still possesses active forces, and everything proclaims that it will use them. The precarious political balance in Hungary is but a respite that has to be turned to advantage.

From Slovakia, the news is bad. Hitler's headquarters have already announced the crushing of the Slovakian insurrection —and soon, desperate messages confirm the news. The partisans are said to have capitulated! It will take several weeks for the details to be known with certainty at Hazalah; a surviving partisan, by the name of Aaron, has succeeded in fleeing and hiding out in Bratislava. He is the sole survivor from his partisan unit. Many partisans, many young Jews, have fallen in combat. Most of their groups have been betrayed. Some Palestine *halutzim* have fallen into the hands of the enemy. There is sadness, but mixed with pride. The Jewish partisans have inflicted heavy losses on the Nazis before succumbing. Their deaths will weigh on the destinies of other men. The ideal of Hazalah has been fulfilled.

"The comrades we have lost so far," writes Rafi ben Shalom, "have disappeared in the fogs of uncertainty. But my comrade Egon died a combatant, killed by a German grenade. We accept his death, for it had a meaning and signified honor."

In Slovakia, the last surviving Jews have been deported "for reasons of military security."

SIXTEEN

Regroupings in Budapest

BLONDE, GRACEFUL, rather flighty, the girl wears a gold chain with a cross around her neck. Chattering away, she doesn't allow any of her travel companions to forget that she is the daughter of an important Hungarian senior officer. She is going to see him, in fact. At the present time he commands a region or a regiment (she doesn't know which exactly—girls aren't very aware of such things) which includes forced-labor conscripts. Jews, she has been told. Some kind of outcasts. Really, how could her father, an officer without a mark against him, be so unlucky?

At Varpalota Station she says good-bye to her new friends. It is early October and, in spite of the cold that comes with nightfall, the girl wears only a light summer coat. She knows it is a detail that could betray her, for she is actually a

Hazalah messenger. But there are no winter coats in Budapest. Another problem is getting rid of too-ardent companions. For that, she has a good line: "My father, the colonel is supposed to come and pick me up; I have a date with him. He's very touchy, and he can't stand young men hanging around. He has a terrible temper . . ."

Once more, things go well; the suitors of the train have departed; the police have not sniffed out her false papers, and the too-light coat has attracted no attention from the secret-police inspectors posted at each station and assigned to uncover Jews traveling against regulations, black marketeers, enemies of the regime . . .

The girl walks quickly; she doesn't even have a contact in town—no room to rest and relax in, to get herself ready for entering the camp. She has to improvise, following as best she can the itinerary that the Hazalah leaders gave her, which is sewn into the lining of her skirt. By nightfall, she arrives in sight of the M.U.S.Z. camp. With a flashlight, a partisan gives her the agreed-upon signal. A little later, she is in the loft of a kind of barn. Three boys greet her joyfully, but not without concern; from various signs, they have the feeling that the guards are on the alert. The rounds are more numerous than usual; the soldiers have conducted surprise searches in the barracks. They do not have much time.

The three partisans: Pinchas Rosenbaum, David Assael, Ossy. The arrival of the Hazalah messenger is the logical outcome of Josy Katz's Budapest escape. It will make the next escape of a group of Jewish partisans possible. Sets of Aryan papers change hands. The signatures and the stamps are perfect; since the first documents by Mimish, the counterfeiters in Budapest have reached a degree of imitation that fools the most punctilious Hungarian officials. Money too: a thousand *pengos.* The boys want to ask the girl many questions. News from their parents, if possible. News from Budapest; how is life there since the "transformation," since Regent Horthy has regained power from the Nazis and stopped the "departures" of the Jews? How does the immediate future look? Is Tijoul still functioning? Are the rumors that Horthy is getting ready to negotiate an armistice confirmed? And victory? Is that near?

They would like just to listen to her talk, because she is a girl, and pretty, and part of the movement. But Pinchas Rosenbaum steps in:

"No more idle talk. Get back to your barracks. And you, you're leaving the camp. Right now . . ."

A partisan sees the messenger off as far as the first houses of the town. Then . . . then she'll walk all night alone, through the empty and hostile streets, eluding the patrols, until the time for the first train to Budapest. Or else she'll try to find a hiding place where she can get some sleep. A clean hideout, because in order to get easily through the police checkpoints at the station she has to make a good appearance—her hair combed, her expression cheerful.

As soon as she has left the barn, a cadre corporal with a flashlight looms up, suspicious. He has seen shadows disappearing in the dark. Have they had a visitor in the barracks?

Pinchas barely has time to sneak the false documents under his pallet. He decides to give up something to avoid a disastrous search: the money. Ostentatiously, he puts his hands behind his back to catch the attention of the corporal. And, stepping back, he draws away from his pallet. The point is to distract the mind and eyes of the soldier as much as possible; to drag out the conversation. Finally, he shows the money and suggests that they share it. The partisans know that the members of the cadre, badly fed and deprived, are corruptible. For when the Jewish conscripts succeed in securing a little money they also secure the silence of the Hungarians.

The corporal demands 500 *pengos*—a considerable amount. But it will save the false papers under the pallet. Pinchas surrenders the money, and the corporal withdraws, asking ironically the date of the "next pay." "These Jews," he thinks, "they're able to get money even in the middle of a labor camp!" Of course he does not know that the money is intended to pay for freedom.

There are two impeccable "sets" of Christian papers; the council of Zionist resistance inside the labor camp has left them for Rosenbaum and Wechter. Everybody tries to assemble some nearly acceptable civilian clothes, sorting through the best articles of clothing from each company. Today, this detail seems funny, but in 1944 the way you were dressed was of great importance. How many messengers were arrested because their threadbare clothes, full of holes, too light for the season, made them objects of police attention. . . . A shoe without a sole or a ragged jacket bespoke the persecuted Jew, the outcast, almost as surely as the mandatory Star of David.

On October 12, at midnight, the two partisans, with their clean shirts, pressed pants, stylish neckties, inch up to the outside wall, ten feet high and topped by barbed wire. The "connection" that had made it possible for the girl to get into the camp is no longer on the job; the corruptible soldier who guaranteed it has been transferred. They have to force their way out.

The partisans are hidden in the shadow, beneath the wall. A human ladder is quickly improvised. Rosenbaum and Wechter hoist themselves to the top and carefully step over the barbed wire. Without hesitation, they jump. They have rehearsed the jump a thousand times, practicing like paratroopers. They do a limber roll-over, and melt into the night.

At the first houses, they stop to catch their breath. Far off, there is the sound of a patrol approaching.

The two partisans put on the caps of the Levente, the paramilitary Hungarian youth organization whose precious badges they have. The cap is usually worn with civilian clothes, so they are easily absorbed into the crowd and—in theory—protected in case of a check. At this time thousands of Leventes are everywhere in Hungary, going from one camp to another, on leave or returning home. The two Jews throw out their chests. They still have to adopt the arrogant manners of the young soldier, his easy hauteur, his limited and slangy vocabulary.

The first stage of the escape is a success; the problem now is to reach Budapest, 70 miles away. Like all Leventes, the partisans will hitchhike. One last test: they recite their new identities to one another, their parents' Christian names, their birth dates, their respective addresses, and everything that concerns the military training camp they are supposed to be coming from. After a final check of papers, money, clothes, they plunge into the universe of the others, of the non-Jews who have the right to move around, to buy a newspaper, to drink a soda, to smoke a cigarette, to laugh with a friend, to live. Their eyes are ill adapted to the light, and their minds to freedom. But it is important not to look scared, anxious, tense, criminal. The two boys station themselves along a highway. The watchword: whatever happens, act like two Hungarian Leventes. Don't ever break this rule.

The bluish headlights of the first truck loom on the horizon; the noise of the engine seems deafening to the boys who feel the strong urge to jump into the ditch, into the darkness from which they have come. But this urge is quickly repressed; like true Leventes, demanding and aggressive, they plant themselves in the middle of the road, arms out. The huge black truck brakes, stops:

"Budapest?"

The driver is visibly furious, but he motions the two boys to climb into the back. They get aboard by hoisting themselves up and parting the greenish camouflage tarp. The truck starts up. Their hearts skip a beat; the truck is full of drowsy SS, German SS! But there is no going back now. The partisans master their surprise—and their fear—and, with an approximation of "gute Nacht," take seats in the only available corner. Almost at once they pretend to be in the deep sleep of the adolescent who has nothing to say, and nothing to answer for.

This chance occurrence, which might have ended so tragically, works to the benefit of the escapees; on the outskirts of Budapest, the German SS truck, including its passengers, gets through all the Hungarian checkpoints. Which of Horthy's police would dare cast a suspicious eye on the elite troop of the Third Reich?

At about four in the morning, taking advantage of a stop the truck makes in the suburbs, the two partisans jump out. With a Hitlerian salute, they take time to thank their indifferent traveling companions. They walk together for a while, then shake hands and separate. Their chances are better alone. In Budapest, two men going about in the night together are even more suspect than one pedestrian alone. Pinchas Rosenbaum goes to the house of one of his cousins, whom the girl messenger has alerted and who lives in a "Jewish house." He has nothing to fear there, for the moment, from the police or even the Gestapo, since the raids and deportations have stopped. He wants to rest, to get the news, before renewing contact with his Hazalah comrades.

The first clandestine meeting Pinchas attends the next day, at 12 Sip Street, enables the partisans to exchange information about the various camps they've escaped from; Josy Katz, Deutsch, Grunwalt, and many others are present.

They all have false identities; for instance, Joseph Katz is

Istvan Dobi, born in Nagyvarad (Transylvania). Their problem is to find a safe shelter and to maintain liaison with Hazalah, for now there is the near certainty that the combat will soon resume, even more viciously than before. Their task is immense: to save lives, to rain heavy blows on the enemy without, however, throwing themselves into hopeless engagements. To break off combat every time the balance becomes too unfavorable, and to take up another form of attack elsewhere, in some other way. To infiltrate the ranks of the enemy. To take risks, but not every risk.

Pinchas Rosenbaum exchanges the Levente uniform he has escaped in for an "Arrow Cross" major's uniform. He shows his comrades the military papers he is carrying. He is no longer the son of the Kisvarda rabbi—dead in Auschwitz—nor the M.U.S.Z. conscript, nor the arrogant Hungarian Levente boy. Now, he is in charge of a Nylas contingent—he is cruel and thirsting for Jewish blood. His comrades look at him with astonishment; even the look in his eyes has changed. His blue eyes, softened by study, made for dreaming, have assumed the hard luster of steel; he has that tight, thin-lipped half-smile of the warrior with no God, no scruples—sadistic, betrothed to death.

"To fight the enemy," he says, "you must look like him. Externally."

SEVENTEEN

After the Nazi Coup d'Etat

ON SUNDAY, October 15, at 1:27 P.M., Radio Budapest broadcasts a proclamation by Horthy announcing that Hungary is ready to capitulate "in order not to serve as a rearguard battlefield of the Reich." In his message, the regent takes pains to stress that the Germans are solely responsible for the persecutions endured by the Jews in the country.

The war is over! There is an outburst of joy. In the streets, processions of excited people form. Jews are seen dancing with joy, yanking off their yellow stars and burning them in public. Are the deportations, the denunciations, the brutalities of the Nazis and the gendarmes truly forgotten? Is the ordeal ended? Do the Hungarian Jews really believe it, or pretend to believe it?

At Hazalah, they do not share the dubious bliss. They

know that the political situation is confused, that there is much to be feared in the events to come, that the Nazis are not going to accept the too predictable turnabout of the regent without some reaction; they will be all the more combative for having been shoved so rudely from power and brought to trial; they are preparing their revenge. And their time, without doubt, is near.

The illusion of peace will last a little less than six hours. Six hours of excitement, expectation; then silence, anxiety. For if the Hungarians know that their country's fate oscillates, the Jews—at least those who resist irrational optimism—are aware that their fate as human beings is at stake. For those in Hazalah who are better informed than the others, more realistic, more farsighted, it is the last calm before the eleventh-hour fight.

Of course, Horthy's message is the topic of every conversation. It is obvious that he is seeking to absolve himself and his country in the eyes of the world of the massacres already perpetrated in Hungary. But what are the practical consequences of his speech? Is the security of the surviving Jews strengthened thereby? Nothing encourages such a belief.

Horthy's speech is only a speech of convenience. And even its sincerity can be doubted. The regent's past is enough to condemn him. His contempt for the Jews has existed throughout his career. His taking of power in 1919 was marked by a "white terror" and a series of bloody pogroms in Siofok, Orgovany, and elsewhere. Did he not enact, as early as 1920, anti-Semitic laws (the first in Europe) and the "restricted quota" in the University? Anti-Semitism runs through his whole career. Baky—today in disgrace—has been one of his faithful companions. No doubt, the regent's contempt for the Jews differs from the implacable hatred the German or Hungarian Nazis bear them. But these feelings once were combined into a common impulse. For the Hazalah young people it is impossible to concede—as Horthy is now trying to make people believe—that the Hungarians have been the playthings of the Germans. The regent's tardy regrets have the appearance of a political maneuver—a vain one.

The regent's determination to pull Hungary out of the war, for the first time asserted publicly on radio, has been known a long time and cannot be doubted. But under scrutiny it takes on a special meaning.

Horthy has been Hitler's irreproachable ally. Motivated by a deep hatred of Soviet Russia, he gave himself unreservedly to the Führer. His loyalty was total, up to the moment he could see clearly the outcome of the conflict. Then, not without reluctance and apprehension, he resolved to negotiate. First he tried to open a dialogue with the Anglo-Saxons. But they made it clear to him that the logical interlocutor, for Hungary, was eastward.

For this painful and difficult mission, the regent has designated his son, young Nicolas Horthy. As early as August, the younger Horthy set about establishing contacts with the Russians (who were slowing their advance into the heart of the country), with Tito's partisans, with the Social Democrats—in short with all the adversaries of the occupying Nazis. But the regent's hesitations and soul-searching do not make the opening of true conferences with the East very easy; his private adviser for Russian affairs, chief of staff Ratcz, loses any hope of reaching a favorable result. A Soviet "contact" having been established, it is decided that a plane should take off secretly from Budapest with a Hungarian delegation, including the younger Horthy. The regent agrees, then refuses, under the pretext that all the airstrips are under Nazi surveillance. They decide, therefore, to take off from the "Field of Blood"—Budapest's military parade grounds. Horthy gives his approval, then, at the last moment, withdraws it. The delegation takes off, but his son remains at his side. And the dealings proceed listlessly—made all the more difficult by Molotov who, from the beginning, sets conditions almost unacceptable for Horthy: a Hungarian army offensive, from the interior, against the Germans, the neutralization of the SS, and, for the future, a return to the borders as they were before the Treaty of Trianon, the Translyvania question for the moment remaining unsolved. Moreover, Horthy's entourage is infiltrated by the Nazis, so that the Arrow Cross and, consequently the Germans, are able to follow, day by day, the meager progress of the talks.

Under analysis, Horthy's position appears quite difficult, fragile, threatened, ambiguous. And of that, the partisans are convinced—a conviction that is at the root of their anxiety. The muffled struggle for power being waged in Hungary these many months seems very dangerous to them, all the more so with the Red Army not advancing as quickly as expected, with the war dragging in the West, with the Reich falling to pieces, bombarded, almost wiped out, but taking so much time to collapse. It is clear, to the surviving Hungarian Jews, that the truce ordained by Horthy and his prime minister, Lakatos, constitutes only a postponement; that the deportations, almost miraculously suspended, can resume at any moment. They know in Budapest that the death camps continue to function in Upper Silesia and elsewhere, that the defeated Nazis, far from abandoning the "final solution," are trying to expedite it so they can use the little time left them to the maximum. It may seem absurd, but it is the reality. The shadow of near, irremediable defeat, instead of curbing the murderous fury of the Nazis, seems to exacerbate it. Into the collective slaughter of innocents, they are about to throw, they are throwing, their last resources and their last strength. The Hungarian Jews who think—and maintain—that the Nazis, beaten on all fronts, hemmed in and threatened by the enemy, will have more pressing concerns from now on than to carry out the massacre, are wrong. The slaughter of Jews will remain to the end their main objective! Such is the conclusion the Hazalah partisans have reached. And coming events, against all logic and all hope, will prove them right.

In dismissing Baky and Endre, his old companions, zealous agents of the Nazis and Hungarian henchmen of extermination, in nominating General Lakatos as prime minister, Horthy has officially shown his hand: armistice, cease-fire, negotiation. The Hungarian Nazis, after having failed in their first attempt to seize power, do not, however, consider themselves beaten. Led by Szalasi, chief of the "Arrow Cross," benefiting of course from the total support of the occupying Germans, they are preparing themselves to seize power. Careful, they group themselves in buildings that are placed under German authority, in barracks occupied by the SS, therefore protected from the Hungarian police. They are the "untouchables" and can quietly work at their coup d'état. Just as everyone in Budapest knows of the negotiations the royal palace is carrying on with the Soviets, so everyone also knows, or foresees, that the Arrow Cross is preparing for a takeover. Lakatos's timid protests have been to no avail; the Germans thoroughly support Szalasi. (Veesenmayer, in early October, brings him a message from Hitler expressing the wish that he soon succeed Horthy.) Nobody doubts that their hour will soon strike.

The Hazalah partisans relax none of their activity: false IDs, Hungarian or neutral, continue to be mass-produced. The protected houses, whose extraterritoriality is legally ascertained, are set up to receive ten times, 50 times more refugees than planned. Elisabeth Eppler, in charge of contacts with the Swiss embassy, manages audaciously to sneak a stack of blank documents out of the embassy.

"President Stern," Elisabeth relates, "had put me in charge of liaison with the Swiss diplomats who represented the American interests at that time in Hungary. I had an appointment with two lady employees of the consulate, the Benedeck sisters. For a few moments, I found myself alone in an office. I took advantage of it to quickly open all the drawers. What concerned me most was the rubber stamp, the American seal. I couldn't find one, but I did manage to sneak some blank passes, meant for people applying for American naturalization. Precious documents. I also brought back Shraga Weil (who became one of the greatest Israeli artists) to the Hazalah secret press installed in a cellar; she went to work immediately. The important thing was to duplicate the documents and, using a model, to copy the seal of the United States of America. Shraga and her crew worked eight days without stopping. Rafi Friedl and other partisans, who had rescue operations in mind, waited impatiently."

Already, Jews without homes, refugees from the provinces begin to crowd the House of Glass on Vadasz Street. The neutral diplomats, especially Raoul Wallenberg, along with representatives of the community like Krausz, study ways to parry any eventual resumption of Nazi action.

The clumsiness of the regent's entourage will hasten events. General Lakatos—never known for his diplomatic skill—issues a note to the Germans, early in October, requesting that they not move any troops without prior approval of Horthy's chiefs of staff. This amounts to declaring openly that the regent has militarily broken off from the occupying authority; it amounts to the creation of an emergency situation for the Nazis, and all the more so because of the resumption of the Soviet advance. The Russian troops, commanded by Malinovski and Tolboukhine, have just crossed the Tisza and have reached Necskemet, 60 miles from Budapest! In both camps—at the royal palace and among the Nazis at the Majestic—room to maneuver shrinks. The Soviets now demand that Horthy immediately proclaim a cease-fire and his intention to capitulate. So warned, the Nazis are ready to reassert control of the situation. For them too, it is the eleventh hour.

The cease-fire proclamation by the regent, supreme head of all Hungarian military operations, is set for October 18. On October 15, a crown council is scheduled to establish the technicalities of the cease-fire and its practical application. Does Horthy really think that he will be able to pull his country out of the war, to spare it the ordeal of defeat? Perhaps even to keep some territorial advantages it owes to the Nazis' friendship and to stay in power, or at least to pass the country on to his son, the designated heir? Impossible to know for certain today. In any case, he acts as though these options were still before him.

Very early in the morning, a radiant sun makes the roofs of Budapest glow and colors the Danube. It is Saint Martin's summer. During the night, messages sent out from the Hungarian headquarters have arrived at the units announcing the imminence of the cease-fire and the end of the alliance with the Nazis. Many partisans who are out in the streets very early—on liaison missions, to "deliver" false papers or neutral-country certificates to ill-hidden and scattered Jews, or even to inspect bunkers and weapons caches—notice a strange agitation among the military. In the M.U.S.Z. camps the atmosphere becomes—suddenly—very cordial. It is fraternization day. The cadre, soldiers and noncoms, become friendly with the Jews—almost protective! At the Franz Josef barracks in Budapest some noncoms go so far as to declare to the Jews, "Now we're on the same side!" and to distribute weapons to them (some will end by being added to the Hazalah arsenal). In one morning, the outcast Jewish conscripts, the forced laborers, and the prisoners become companions in arms to their Hungarian executioners . . .

The reason for this turnabout is plain: Horthy's chiefs of

staff foresee that the announcement of capitulation will bring the German army of occupation up against the Hungarian forces. A private strategic plan has been in the works for a month. The guard of the royal palace—the impregnable fortress that dominates Budapest—has been reinforced. Liaison with the Hungarian armies assured (in reality, they are controlled by Nazi agents), the divisions engaged against the Russians are alerted. Twelve miles from Budapest, an elite corps of a thousand Hungarian troops, well armed, with vehicles, is ready to intervene. All forces had been placed under the command of General Bakay, who is faithful to the regent. Bakay is kidnaped October 10 by the Germans. Under the command of his successor, General Aggeteliky, the plan in broad outline has not changed; it remains based upon a resistance of several days—time enough for the Soviets to pierce the front and arrive in Budapest. At the same time, the two main Hungarian armies in operation in the Carpathians (one under General Miklos, one under General Veress) will rally to the Soviets and aid them in pursuing the Germans. . . . According to the men around Horthy, the effect of surprise will facilitate the working out of the "secret plan," for which they seek all the help they can get, even among the Jewish conscripts. The Germans, caught short, will flee to the Austrian border.

The reality is quite different. The Hungarian Nazis are apprised of everything and in control, down to the minutest detail, of Horthy's about-face. At the royal palace, even in the anteroom of the naïve and conspiratorial old regent (he is 75), they have zealous and efficient agents. As early as September, the Nazis have dispatched to Budapest two of their best troubleshooters, Skorzeny, still wearing the halo won for rescuing Mussolini at Grand Sasso, and SS General Bach Zelewski, victor over the Warsaw insurgents. The general has brought with him a huge mortar that has proved itself in Poland and Sevastopol. With the two men, German units have quietly entered the capital. The Hazalah partisans have observed these movements, not without concern, as have the men around Horthy; in early October, the Tenth Hungarian Infantry Division has been recalled from the Carpathians. Another is to follow. The allies of yesterday are really clearing the field for action. For one side as for the other, there is no going back.

On Sunday, the 15th, from early dawn events rush onward, contradictory at first, undecipherable, then dramatic. While unexpected scenes of fraternization between Hungarian soldiers and Jewish conscripts take place in the city and at camp, the crown council—no doubt one of the most important in the history of the nation—prepares itself. It is 8:45 A.M. Shortly before nine young Nicolas Horthy receives a phone call: Tito's emissaries, with whom he has been having difficult negotiations for weeks, make an appointment with him in Pest for 10 o'clock, on the third floor of an apartment overlooking a square near the Danube. He accepts the appointment; he leaves, accompanied by three bodyguards and followed by an army detachment, at the same time the counselors, grave and preoccupied, are getting ready to meet. The car arrives at the place the "partisans" have chosen, at the intersection of two empty streets. To lull the suspicion of the Hungarians, the Nazis have disguised several men as Jews; they flaunt the yellow star. The younger Horthy gets out of the car, all unsuspecting; he is assaulted immediately. Caught in the trap, he defends himself bravely, supported by his guard, while his men, with the help of grenades, try to release him. But Skorzeny, who leads the operation in person, intervenes. Wounded, young Nicolas Horthy is captured; they throw him, rolled up inside a Persian rug, into the back of a truck. One of his guards is dead, another seriously wounded, as is the chauffeur. Miraculously, the third guard manages to flee. He will be caught (and clubbed) by the Gestapo men, wearing the Star of David, in a telephone booth nearby. But in the meantime he has had time to inform the palace.

Distraught, the regent opens the crown council one hour late, at 11. Under the emotional shock caused by the arrest of his son, he decides to proclaim the armistice immediately rather than wait till the 18th of October, the original date. But before the rereading of the text—and its broadcast over the radio—Veesenmayer, Hitler's ambassador, is announced at the palace. Horthy, with his counselors, receives Veesenmayer and tells him the decision that has just been taken: capitulation. Veesenmayer savagely counterattacks; he declares that the regent's son has been caught in the act of treason: he had made an appointment with the partisans. Horthy, who understands the trap set for his son, vainly protests. Veesenmayer takes his leave.

Shortly afterward, the regent signs the text of his proclamation and gives the order that it be broadcast as soon as possible. It is almost 1 o'clock when Rahn, Hitler's ambassador extraordinary, is announced. The city, says Rahn, is under the threat of destruction. Perhaps he mentions the possibility of some secret weapon in the possession of Hitler which can turn the tide of the war. No doubt he adds threats concerning Nicolas. Prostrate, frightened, his nerves frayed, the old regent promises to postpone his decision, to take his place once again on the side of the Axis. But his proclamation has already been broadcast over Radio Budapest. The Nazi response is not long in coming.

At Hazalah, as elsewhere, of course, no one knows about these shifts in events. But, as early as three in the afternoon, organization watchmen signal the first demonstrations of the "Arrow Cross" in the streets. The Germans have brought in truckloads of youths dressed in green shirts and fully armed, chanting slogans against the regent and his entourage, demanding a mass levy against the Russians and death to the spared Jews. Toward 4:30, German troops occupy the Hungarian radio station.

At the royal palace, around the bewildered, broken Horthy, powerless counselors try without real conviction to implement the scheduled resistance plan in opposition to the Nazi takeover, which begins to take shape early in the afternoon. But coded orders destined for the army no longer get through; they are intercepted by officers planted by the Nazis at the transmission center. General Aggeteliky, as faithful to the regent as was his predecessor Bakay, is arrested by his own adjutant. Chief of Staff Janos Voros is said to have gone over to the Nazi camp (the news will be denied). Then communications are interrupted; the royal palace is isolated.

However, Hazalah observers take note of developments in the coup d'état. On Theresa Boulevard, Josy Katz sees the German troops crossing the Danube from east to west. Not far from Laudon Street, he meets Pinchas Rosenbaum and David Assael—who has also escaped—on a reconnaissance mission. The bits of information they have fit together; it is indeed a Nazi takeover. A meeting is scheduled for the Hazalah scouts—in case of sudden danger, at 29 Vadasz Street.

At 6:30, the Germans officially turn power over to the Szalasi team. The first move of the new leader is to go to the radio station. At 7 o'clock, an announcer issues a proclamation of the "National Guide" of the Arrow Cross: the war will be carried out against the Soviets in the name of "the fear of God and the teaching of the Christ." An order of the day follows from the new commander in chief, ordering the Hungarian military fighting the Red Army to continue the battle. At the same time, posters go up on the walls of Budapest: the curfew is set for 9 P.M. The Hazalah messengers make haste. A new radio communiqué announces a series of measures concerning the Jews; they are forbidden to leave the houses assigned to them! Any Jew found in the streets will be shot on sight.

Around 8 o'clock shooting breaks out in Pest, on the left bank of the Danube, where the overwhelming majority of the Jews are, especially in the "ghetto" around the synagogue. The Hazalah leaders have to proceed on the assumption that the Arrow Cross has not waited for the day to end before resuming their hunt for Jews, interrupted now for several months. They decide to put their emergency plan into operation. Just before the curfew, messengers are rushed with false papers to threatened Jews in different parts of Pest. At the intersection of Kiraly and Dob streets, Josy Katz arrives just in time to save a Jewish family by leading it into a protected house. The Arrow Cross is on his heels. But other messengers are intercepted before or during rescue operations and are shot down. At nightfall, Jewish blood flows in the streets of Budapest.

Hazalah mobilizes. The watchword: keep calm, do not get involved in hopeless fights, and take shelter. Some Jewish groups, partly Hazalah partisans and partly Social Democratic workers, unable to contain themselves or to calm their itch to get into the fight, make a stand against the enemy. At 31 Nepszinhaz Street and at 4 Telecki Square, they barricade themselves with a few guns and grenades, and they start a fight with the Arrow Cross, who are walking the streets in search of victims. Several Nazis are killed; the others rush off looking for reinforcements. In the night, the two islands of resistance are ringed by elite German troops supported by several Tiger tanks, the guns of which go on firing till morning. On Nepszinhaz Street the Nazis take a few prisoners to the Dohany Street synagogue, where they are executed. Women and children share the same fate at the Tattersall, the riding club, on Telecki Square. No one surrenders; Jews, boys and girls, exhaust their ammunition and let themselves be exterminated as, long before, in Massada. History has not even preserved their names. When all resistance is quashed, in early morning, the Germans hammer away at the buildings and destroy them completely.

The Hazalah partisans are severely critical of such isolated actions. In spite of the respect that the desperate heroism of these Jews inspires in them, they disapprove of their suicide action. With all their strength they believe, they want to believe, in a plan of concerted action, in a method, and in calculating the odds. They will not face the enemy as martyrs but as combatants, masters of their destiny who have weighed their chances. Such has been, till this tragic day, the meaning of their action. Now that the Nazis have regained power, the Budapest Zionists will be able to evaluate the merits of their expectations and the efficacy of their method. Three months of terror in Pest, four in Buda will give its full meaning to Operation Hazalah.

EIGHTEEN

The Massacres Begin

AT DAWN on October 16, scouts on a surveillance mission send word that German troops and well-armed Nylas militiamen, brought in by truck, encircle the Budapest seventh district where the isolated engagements of the day before took place. Soon, what seems a crucial raid begins. Roused from sleep, Jews are thrown into the street, with no distinction as to age and sex. They're allowed no luggage; blows and commands fall thick and fast. It's clear that the occupying Germans and their Hungarian allies who have just seized power have been ordered to act with the utmost dispatch! Perhaps they are afraid that other hotbeds of resistance will spring up in the city, that the Jews will launch another desperate uprising, as in Warsaw.

Near Telecki Square, the wreckage under which the combatants have allowed themselves to be buried is still smoking; Josy Katz witnesses some appalling scenes. Pummeled by rifle butts, Jews are assembled, hands over heads, in the middle of the street. Those who don't move quickly enough, the aged, the sick, underfed and terrorized children, are shot down on the spot before the eyes of the others. An old woman who tries to talk things over with a young Hungarian in green shirt and tawny boots receives a blow from his rifle butt which literally opens her face. A little girl who bends over her is shot down by the burst of a machine gun. From where he is hiding, Katz hears the cries of despair, the death rattles.

There are perhaps a thousand of them being clubbed and rushed off to deportation. From other streets come other pitiable processions of the condemned. Soon, guns going off and machine guns rattling echo everywhere. All day the Hazalah partisans try in vain to count the victims.

Meanwhile, the radio broadcasts alarming news: the Jews of Budapest are confined to their homes for ten days. No aid for the sick; no burials. Mixed marriages are declared invalid. Men and women 16 to 60 years old will be taken to the front for work on military installation. (But age distinctions are seldom respected by the police.) "Thus the Jews will participate in the effort to contain the Communist tide—which they have provoked and fostered!" declares the announcer.

Events unfold faster than expected. In the various Hazalah centers, messengers' reports accumulate, and they all refer to the same murderous fury. People are slaughtered in the middle of the street in broad daylight. Killed for nothing. The rare news they get from the provinces is also tragic. On the nights of the 15th and 16th of October, innumerable murders are committed; hordes of Nylas stormed everywhere. In the M.U.S.Z., full companies of Jewish conscripts who had fraternized with the Hungarians are put before the firing squad. Now that the Arrow Cross is in power, its press is triumphant: "Glorious Days Are Here Again," is the headline of the party's official organ, *Harc* ("combat"). Another daily paper (*Maggyarsag*) mentions—small comfort—insurrectionary outbursts in Budapest: "Jews shoot at German soldiers. Their crime is an insult to God. Till now their punishment has been moderate."

Hazalah's motto remains: don't yield to panic. Foreseeably, the takeover will stir up a vengeful fury. But things will ease, relatively, and the situation, hopefully, should soon become more propitious for a true counterstroke. Hazalah's emphasis is on self-control.

Not so at the royal palace. The regent's entourage is at wit's end. Tremendous confusion, it becomes known much later, prevails all night. There is no news from the two generals at the borders, on whom the "secret" plan of resistance has rested. With no communication, the royal palace is like a ship without a rudder in a raging storm. Skorzeny—Skorzeny again—will lead the boarding party. At dawn a German column forms at the foot of the palace hill. During the night—as a token of appeasement, or friendship—the Hungarian army has removed the mines, at the request of the Germans. The German column, led by Skorzeny and followed by four heavy tanks and some light Goliaths brim full of explosives, runs into no problems reaching the Vienna gate, and then the summit of the palace hill. The Hungarian garrison, taken by surprise, outbluffed, does nothing. The only fighting occurs in the gardens. Total dead, seven; wounded, 26. The column undertakes a pincers movement, surrounds the war ministry building where a thousand men stand by, arms at the ready, and Hitler's henchman reaches Horthy's apartments, inside the huge brick-walled citadel.

The regent is no longer there; warned only a few minutes

before, he has taken refuge at SS General Wildenbruch's—onetime friend of the kaiser. That is where he will sign—three hours later—his abdication and the resignation of his government. In three days he leaves for Germany, under the escort of Skorzeny. But in the meantime Szalasi's government is made official; one of its first acts, after the enactment of new measures against the Jews, is to denounce Hungary's capitulation.

The triumph of Szalasi and the Arrow Cross is celebrated in Budapest for the next several days by dreadful human sacrifices. That such hideous scenes could have taken place in our time, in familiar surroundings; that the men and women who survived were witnesses to them and today keep these recollections engraved in their memories, is almost beyond belief. And whoever tries, with the insufficient perspective of a third of a century, to reconstitute these scenes wonders whether he is reporting real facts or describing a nightmare.

Unfortunately, figures don't lie; you can always count the dead, even those without graves.

Ferenczy, the sinister police lieutenant colonel, the child murderer, receives a promotion, his reward for hatred; from now on he is the commissioner of Jewish affairs, in charge of enforcing the new measures; he exceeds them, ordering his men, and the Nylas groups attached to them, to exterminate on the spot any Jew caught in a violation of the rules. The terminology of the new authorities is a measure of their cruelty: "Any Jew caught outside will be 'cut into four pieces' (in Hungarian, *Felkoncolni*)," as a poster later plastered on the walls announces.

The streets are full of armed men, mostly young men, in green shirts and black pants, their red brassards marked with the arrow cross in a white circle, who have no other mission than to hunt down Jews, no other command than to unmask those hiding under false identities, to shoot down on sight anyone who trespasses against the new regulations, or to "clean out" certain districts suddenly declared, as fancy dictates, strategic zones (meaning places in which Jews have no right to reside, although they are assigned there by law and forbidden to leave for ten days). Isolated individuals, groups, families, whose behavior or appearance seems dubious, are taken to Nylas stations. Men are submitted to the physical check: if they are circumcised, it means instant death. Often, women are tortured because the exterminators also seek the famous Jewish "treasures." Corpses are thrown into the Danube, which at certain points, between Pest and Buda, is nearly three-quarters of a mile wide.

In the face of this blind fury, Hazalah renews its pleas for self-control, but gives the green light to the rescue commandos. As early as October 16, partisans embark upon the dreadful merry-go-round of death. Against the spreading terror, in the face of the Tommy guns sputtering everywhere, they have only feeble weapons at their disposal: the neutral protection certificates, the false "Schutzpasses," manufactured in haste on the clandestine press at the Swiss house on Vadasz Street. Orphans are taken in and provided with Aryan papers. The Hungarian police, the Nylas, the pro-Nazi militia bear (but for how much longer?) a certain respect for these documents, written in Hungarian, with German and French translations, and carrying the seals and stamps of foreign powers. In any case, for the moment, there is nothing else to do; an armed uprising would be crushed in a few hours.

Emmeric Deutsch is assigned the mission of giving aid, in whatever way he can, to Jewish orphans between eight and 12 years old who have been brought together in a hospital. There is no way to give each of them a Schutzpass. Perhaps negotiation is possible; it entails considerable risk for the messenger, but how can one accept the death of defenseless children? Hazalah gets word that the orphanage is about to be raided at any minute, and the children wiped out.

Deutsch gets there too late; flanked by Arrow Cross men, the children are already being walked down the street in the midst of an indifferent crowd. Deutsch can do nothing but mix with the onlookers. At one point, a child, taking fright or recognizing a familiar face, breaks rank and begins to run. A Nylas calmly puts a bullet in his back. The crowd moves away from the dead little body. Deutsch remains still. One gesture would betray him, and he has ten certificates in his pocket.

Efra and Pil—Tijoul survivors—have managed to get uniforms and papers of senior Hungarian railroad employees. It is a good cover; often during the day, Efra successfully crosses the closely guarded bridges over the Danube between Buda and Pest. They step up the rescue missions. During a raid, Efra, drawing near a Jewish house with the intention of giving papers to an endangered family, is suddenly identified by an Aryan Hungarian who bears him no particular grudge.

"So now you're station master, you filthy Jew!"

Public denunciation of this sort equals a death sentence. A crowd gathers. Efra sees a ring of hostile faces. Fists are brandished.

"Let's go get the Nylas! Let's take him to the police . . ."

Whatever he says, whatever papers he produces, Efra feels the jaws of the vise tighten. If he is done for, at least he will try to save his comrade who is wearing the same uniform. He grabs him:

"You bastard! You turned me in . . ."

But the Hungarians aren't fooled.

"They're Jews, both of them! The bastards!"

Drawn by the noise, two Nylas brutes armed to the teeth

elbow their way through the crowd. Revolvers out, they demand that the Jewish spies be turned over to them at once, and they begin giving them a violent beating, punching and kicking them. Efra and his companion, gasping, follow the Nylas while fending off the crowd. They have no illusions as to the fate awaiting them. This mission will be their last. Their executioners drag them, according to habit, toward the river.

They do not go very far—a hundred yards or so. The two Arrow Cross apologize for having been a little too rough. They are themselves two Zionist youths from Hazalah—Zall and Willi—on a rescue mission! They have to part quickly, because they are in the middle of a raid, and other Arrow Cross patrols—real ones—are all over the place in this district; the two prisoners could be claimed for a mass execution. The incident has lasted a few minutes. Time enough for Efra and his companion to dry the streams of blood from their faces, to fix their clothes, and resume their "work."

In this storm, every successful mission is a miracle, for the risks are immense. But calls for help multiply. And in the Hazalah message centers, where intelligence is gathered, the staff tries to keep up.

In Budapest, few are the Jews who, when preparing for the Friday evening Sabbath, escape the feeling that they are lighting the lights for the last time. From all sides, the menace grows, tightens. On the radio—to which the Jews are forbidden to listen—incitements to murder follow one upon the other, in a tone sometimes bordering on hysteria.

"But what have we done?" a little Jewish boy asks his father, in a house surrounded by the hatred.

"We made a mistake," is the answer. "We thought there was such a thing as justice. And also innocence . . ."

None of this keeps the president of the Misrahi (religious) Zionist movement, Eugene Frankel, from going on with his preparation for the service. Nor is it too hard for him to prepare for the death he knows he faces. What is hard is to answer the questions the children ask him. He has just been released by the Hungarian Gestapo. In the jail cells at the Little Majestic, then in the cellars of Foe Street, for weeks he has undergone endless torture and questioning. He has seen many Jewish Resistance prisoners there, in those sinister basements—Dr. Siegfried Roth, Dr. Sweiger, among others; he does not know what happened to them. His own release came as a surprise. The only explanation he can come up with is the enforcement of the general plan of extermination: Since all Jews are condemned, the Nazis have no time to waste on individual cases. In any event, he has arranged a hideout, pitiful though it is, in the back of his apartment. His premonition is soon borne out. On the night after the Sabbath he is wakened by an uproar coming from the concierge's quarters, then footsteps on the stairway. Finally, shouts of "Hey, Jew Frankel! Open up."

On the landing is the concierge, his face bleeding, flanked by a plainclothesman and four armed Nylas, their caps adorned by little plumes, arrow crosses on their brassards. They yell at Frankel, "Get moving, you Jew bastard . . . and no luggage."

In the half-darkness, Frankel thinks he is suffering from hallucinations; one of the young Nazis, his face distorted by hate and fury, looks like a young partisan from the Misrahi movement—Pinchas Rosenbaum, the son of the Kisvarda rabbi. Frankel hasn't time to think about it; brutalized, shaken, half-stunned, dragged down the stairway, he is thrown into the rear of an olive-drab Gestapo car that starts off like a shot, leaving the concierge quivering, paralyzed. A little later, at the House of Glass, the commando pioneers—Pinchas Rosenbaum, Brener Loeffler, David Klein, and his brother, called "Little Skull," explain:

"We had to act fast because the real detachment out to arrest you was right behind us. We also had to get rough, because we knew that the concierge had his eye on you, and that one error, the slightest sign of recognition, would have tipped him off. Now, he'll be able to swear, without lying, that you have already been arrested, and by true Nylas . . ."

"Little Skull," arrested by true Nylas, in the course of another mission, will soon after be taken to the Isle of Csepel, a port on the Danube, today the site of a big steel mill. Loeffler succeeds in getting him out of prison by a grandiose scheme: using a number of phone calls and a set of false papers, he manages to pass himself off as the Swiss ambassador! The two comrades resume their rescue operations and pursue them until December. Many Hungarian Jews owe them their lives. It is not known whether they were arrested together, slaughtered together, or separately. One day the partisans wait for both of them in vain, and there is never again a trace of them.

On Vadasz Street, Eugene Frankel continues to work till the city's liberation, manufacturing false documents and organizing rescue missions.

Prodigiously attentive to the enemy's weaknesses and ready to exploit them, the Hazalah partisans have for a long time observed that the Hungarian Nazis are split into a sizable number of different (and sometimes rival) movements, political factions, paramilitary organizations, police, militia, and auxiliaries like the Kiskas, all receiving their orders from touchy chiefs, each of whom is jealous of his own authority. Of course, the hunt for Jews and Communist spies is their common task. But their strategies differ, as well as their hierarchies and their distinctive insignia. From the beginning, Hazalah hasn't hesitated to create "special commandos" of Arrow Cross. Certainly, the game is dangerous;

they must manage to infiltrate the operating groups, to make themselves felt, sometimes even to frighten people. They must rival the others in apparent cruelty, political enthusiasm, murderous delirium. They must instill a faintheartedness in their opponents in order to dominate them and act with freedom. So, more or less fanciful uniforms make their appearance, for "special groups" of surveillance commandos, arrest commandos, clean up commandos; these uniforms are put together as circumstances dictate and are worn by the boldest—and also the least typical racially—of the partisans. One sometimes sees Pinchas, who has blond curly hair and blue eyes, leave Vadasz Street in a black uniform recalling both an elite German soldier and an Arrow Cross policeman. Or he is a Levente, but with the party insignia! As for Weiskopf, alias Horak, he has created a fictitious Red Cross section. His group has its headquarters at 4 Merleg Street, under the protection of a sign reading "International Red Cross." Wearing black boots, black jodhpurs, a fur-collared black coat, a gray hat, and an undecipherable brassard on which the arrow cross is mixed with the Helvetic cross, he presents himself as a kind of Nazi in the service of the international organization. Furnished with summonses, he resolutely enters Jewish houses and has the confined whose names appear on his documents turned over to him. Most of the time, the concierge (or the person in charge) obeys, intimidated or afraid to be taken as a protector of the Jews in the eyes of an official wearing Nylas insignia. The rescued Jews are immediately taken to a protected house, or some safer shelter.

Under the same cover, Weiskopf increases the number of liaison missions between the protected houses; he brings a few groceries to the famished; he visits the Jewish houses, the "bunkers," the regrouping centers for arrested Jews, the labor camps. He is accompanied by other Red Cross "officials" who are there to protect him in case of need, or at least to inform the network of his arrest. He travels through the suburbs to maintain contact with the Jews who, as early as November 16, are at work on the "military installations." With others disguised as Nylas—Grunwalt, Rosenbaum, among them—he even gets into the Old Buda brickyard where thousands of Jews are jammed together, awaiting deportation. (Thanks to Red Cross orders, Schutzpasses, and fake summonses, they succeed in removing some of the condemned from the death trains.) Their work, in the early days of the terror, also consists in supplying ammunition to the bunkers where the partisans are dug in, with their weapons. One of these missions almost ended in tragedy—because of a hole in a pocket:

"I was going from Vadasz Street to my office on Merleg," recounts Weiskopf, "with a supply of small-arms ammunition. Other partisans, disguised as Red Cross officials, had the job of distributing it. The streets were full of sharp-eyed militia, looking for trouble, on the alert. The important thing was to act as domineering as they did. It was almost noon, on Josef Boulevard, when suddenly I felt the lining of one of my pockets give out; bullets fell to the sidewalk, under the feet of the passersby. Instant panic. Someone was on me at once, pointing to the bullets rolling all over the place. I had an inspiration:

" 'Give me a hand!' I commanded. 'I have to take these to the police. These are bullets confiscated from Jews.'

"I don't know whether or not he believed me—or had seen the bullets come out of my pocket. He hesitated a moment, then, without a word, he squatted down next to me. Fortunately, no Nylas were going by at that precise time. No sooner was everything picked up than I bounded onto the runningboard of a streetcar trundling past in slow motion. The ammunition was saved. And so was I. . . ."

Coça Grunwalt works at the same would-be Red Cross

center on Merleg Street. Hazalah puts him in charge of rescuing women who, like the men, have been requisitioned to work on installations meant to stop the Red Army advance. The "female workers," from 16 to 60 years old, are concentrated in Kissok Stadium. They are taken there by streetcar—and it's during this ride that Grunwalt and the partisans accompanying him distribute the Schutzpasses in the names of those whom they'd been able to contact beforehand (the photograph—a detail that singularly complicates the work—must appear on the Schutzpass). To some who have no photographs, Grunwalt offers Red Cross "papers," or even false summonses from the Nylas police or the Gestapo. The essential thing is to snatch these women from the circuit that ends more often in death than in forced labor. Many of them, however, refuse the Hazalah papers, through fear of provocation, or preferring to stay within the law. For the partisans, it is one more reason to despair; give them a chance for salvation, and, oblivious, the condemned refuse to seize it.

One of Grunwalt's most active companions in these missions is little Billitzer who acts as bodyguard for him and serves as relay for the most dangerous actions. But one day, he fails to keep a date in the Museum Gardens that Grunwalt has made with him. Deep in thought, Grunwalt walks down Emperor William Avenue when he catches sight of a group on the opposite sidewalk: two policemen with Billitzer in tow; his face is almost unrecognizable from the beating he has received. Such a scene has become so frequent in Budapest that passersby don't even turn to look. One of the policemen is carrying Billitzer's briefcase. Grunwalt knows what it contains: blank Schutzpasses and neutral-legation rubber stamps. Has Billitzer caught his comrade's eye? If so, he has read fierce determination in it: you're not alone, nor abandoned to your fate! Grunwalt decides to attempt anything to save Billitzer. He calls a meeting of the partisans.

They have to find out where his comrade has been taken. That is relatively easy, for the "Swiss" group has police contacts. Billitzer is at the Gestapo being tortured. But he denies everything; he maintains that he works for the Red Cross. A rescue operation is organized: they will go, as Gestapo officers, to pick up Billitzer. They are too late; he is already locked up. And he still refuses to talk. Grunwalt will rescue him anyway, thanks to a whole arsenal of Swiss documents, and the help of a high Red Cross official and fake phone calls from the legation!

Billitzer, very shaken by the torture, joins a team of "counterfeiters" located on Josef Boulevard. Grunwalt resumes his rescue missions, and on such a scale that, at Hazalah, they start joking about how he won't work any other way than wholesale—that is, a thousand false documents minimum. The terror is at its height, but the condemned Jews are not beyond a smile or two. Against the rampaging enemy, their weapons are almost nonexistent, their shelters precarious. But they have, even then, their heroes, these Zionists who, like the Zealots of yore when Judea was being attacked by Rome, assume the face of the enemy the better to fight him; these youths whose audacity is without limit—Grunwalt, Weiskopf, Zall, Willi, Deutsch, Humwaldt, Rosenbaum, and many others—who stand up to the adversary on his own ground, with his weapons, and survive. During the first days of the Szalasi terror, the Hazalah partisans stand as pledges for hope.

NINETEEN

Rescue Commandos

AT 24 Dob Street, the "Jewish house" belonging to the consistory harbors numerous families jammed into narrow rooms, without water, almost without food. The concierge keeps his tenants under continuous blackmail. With threats, he makes them give up their last food supplies, their last sweaters, and the few cans of condensed milk that the partisans, at great risk, are sometimes able to bring to the mothers with large families.

To the partisans, this is a very unsafe zone; the Nylas patrol it as if it were occupied territory, and they have no hesitation in entering, under the slightest pretext, the houses marked by the Star of David. The parallel streets Dob and Sip and the cross-street Sebestyen Rumbach enclose a heavily Jewish quarter, containing the grand consistory's synagogue and many others. Raids go on constantly. Under this constant harassment, the arrival of a squad of police raises hardly a stir. On October 18, at lunch time, Zionist commandos under Nylas officer Pinchas Rosenbaum encircle Dob Street.

The aim of the surprise attack is to "arrest" Mr. Tauber, ritual-wine merchant of the community, who is confined to his house, at number 24. His arrest—the real one—is imminent. Hazalah is determined to save him. With the usual threats, the noisy group demands that the janitor turn the Jew Tauber over to them. The warrant, duly stamped by the Vadasz Street specialists raises no suspicion (the doorman has seen many of them; he knows one when he sees one), and the wine merchant is rudely taken in tow.

"Filthy Jew, we'll have your hide . . ."

The first phase is a success, but the operation isn't over; they still have to get the arrested Jew out of the area, which is infested by Nazis who can claim him—something that has often happened. For instance, one may say, "We're on our way back, pals, give us your Jew—we'll liquidate him along with ours . . ."

That is when one must have an answer and avoid raising suspicion. Sometimes the best method is take the offensive: "Hi there, give us your prisoners . . ."

"No! Every man for himself . . . we all have to have our fun!"

Girls, most of all, raise delicate problems. Terrorized, worn out, their nerves frayed, they are nonetheless favored prey on whom the Nylas often sate their savage appetites. Sometimes the partisans must open fire to protect them.

Tauber and the Rosenbaum commandos arrive safely at a protected house. But that same day Pauli, at the head of a group of would-be Gestapo civil employees, lives through a dramatic adventure. His mission is to remove at any cost, from a starred house, a young woman who has desperately called for Hazalah assistance. Pauli chooses dusk, to limit the risks of identification (the partisans are most fearful of the classmate or army friend who will suddenly point at a "Nazi policeman" and shout, "Hey, Weiskopf! or Mayer! or Deutsch!). When he gets to the house, Pauli rings the bell, greets the janitor with a loud "Long live Szalasi!" and, handing him the Gestapo warrant, asks for the young woman, mispronouncing her name on purpose.

But something unexpected happens; the janitor has just received orders from the Nylas police to keep a very close watch on this particular tenant. This Gestapo move seems unacceptable to him. Sensing the situation—a partisan has to have quick reflexes—Pauli yells that all the janitor has to do is to come with them to the Nylas police if he wants to assure himself of the full powers of the Gestapo. Convinced, the janitor goes and gets his tenant; she collapses into sobs when she sees the three abusive plainclothesmen waiting for her. But the man also accepts their offer and dogs the steps of the Jewish group which, not especially happy, heads for 5 Vigyazo Ferenc Street, location of the Arrow Cross police! Fast action is called for; without exchanging a word, the two Zionists accompanying Pauli are of one mind. On the pretext of having another secret arrest mission, they head off in another direction. At least they'll be able to tell other Zionists. The janitor is taken aback; he goes up to Pauli, the group chief, who has the prisoner by the arm. Flight? That would be to sign the young woman's death warrant. Arrested, she'd be tortured for being a possible accomplice. . . . Pauli has to go through with it. And they arrive at the Nylas police station. He realizes that his only hope now lies in determination. Hailing the guard with a loud "Long live Szalasi!" he presents himself to the Nylas officer: "The Hungarian Gestapo and the party are united in the same fight. Your man wants to keep the Gestapo from seizing this Jewish spy!"

The warrant he presents is above suspicion. But the Nylas palaver and cover for their agent.

"That's enough," says the partisan. "Give me the telephone. I'll call Gestapo commandant Eppler, and he'll get in touch with your chief. You'll never hear the end of this . . ."

Later, the fake policeman is to confess that this spontaneous bluff went beyond the limits of his own control; if the Nylas had agreed, he would have called his comrade Elisabeth Eppler at the House of Glass on Vadasz Street. As she spoke German, she would have understood the situation—perhaps—and perhaps answered, "The commandant will be back any minute now, he'll be told and do what is required." In the case of an evasive answer, or even of hesitation, the two Jews—fake policeman and fake detainee—would have been shot on the spot.

Happily, the Nylas officer prefers to settle the matter without having such a high-ranking officer intervene, even by telephone. He repeats that the janitor had only been obeying orders, but he takes upon himself the release of the Jewish woman to the "Gestapo." The partisan signs a release with a show of arrogance and is back in the street with the prisoner. He walks along a while, not saying a word, till he is certain that no one is following him. Then, suddenly, in the total darkness (imposed by the blackout) he dives into a porte-cochère with his prisoner. As she prepares to defend herself, fearing rape, he makes his identity known. The poor thing almost swoons with emotion. Within a few minutes, she has experienced the certainty of approaching death, the prospect of torture, the fear of rape, and finally a return to hope in a way she least expected. As soon as she calms down, she and the would-be Gestapo agent are again on their way. Their destination, the Swiss embassy, Liberty Square. A symbol: a small square, the road to it booby-trapped with mortal dangers.

The raids go on. Men and women from 16 to 60, who had first been confined in the Jewish houses, are regrouped in Kissok Stadium or in the Old Buda brickyard, before leaving for the "installations," which, in the suburbs of the city, are supposed to stop the advance of the Red Army. Eichmann and his staff have moved back into their apartments at the Majestic. In spite of the struggle being waged inside the Gestapo between Himmler (who is ready to negotiate with the Allies and eventually to spare the last of the Hungarian Jews) and Kaltenbrunner (who intends to carry to its conclusion the "final solution"), Eichmann meticulously prepares to resume deportations. The Szalasi government gives him every assurance; has it not recently announced that it no longer recognizes, for the Jew traitors, the protection of the neutral embassies? The danger even focuses on the 10,000 Jews (the number will soon grow) who crowd into the protected houses, placing all their trust in their safe-conducts, and the commitment of the brave consuls, Wallenberg and Lutz. Actually, the protected houses have rapidly become command posts; Hazalah has transferred its nerve centers there.

Swift action is a primary factor, for the city swarms with informers, provocateurs, bounty hunters. What proof is there that some of them—for all the strict internal security—have not infiltrated the House of Glass and other neutral grounds? Very often, Hazalah plays on audacity and surprise. And often audacity and surprise win.

Witness the amazing operation that allows many condemned Jews to be saved, as they are already jammed into the last of the deportation trains, about to leave the brickyard. The Germans have taken possession of the victims the police have delivered to them. They are about to shut the doors. Among the deportees is Deri. He has not lost hope. But soon the hope is reduced to the glimmer of light that filters through the sliding door. . . . He is unable to see a certain plainclothesman having a discussion with the SS officer; the plainclothesman is a high official of the Swiss embassy, whose car, with its pennant, has just parked along the platform. A group of armed Nylas escorts him. He has come to claim those under Swiss "protection. . . ."

Already, policemen are running up and down the platform; they open sliding doors. "Anyone with a Schutzpass get out!"

The crowd stirs, but no one steps down. No one, in the train, has such a document.

But the Arrow Cross—actually partisans—stick their heads inside the cars: "We are Jews! Show us any kind of Hungarian document, and jump out, quick."

A few men understand and follow Deri onto the platform, brandishing an ID card, a marriage certificate, a sports license, anything at all. A would-be Nylas leader pretends to examine the document, declares it valid, under the nose of the German officer, who bows and points to a waiting line for the "protected." Encouraged, many Jews try their luck with the most incongruous of papers: gas bills, commutation tickets, even commercial flyers, which they have hastily picked up inside the cars. The fake Nylas validate whatever is presented to them. When the train starts off, 50 Jews leave the station, flanked by the spurious Arrow Cross. Duration of the operation: ten minutes. Only tight scheduling (the presence of a single Hungarian policeman or senior officer would have been disastrous) has made it possible—and luck too. For it to fail, only one of the SS need have spoken or read Hungarian. And there were many Swabian Hungarians, practically bilingual, in the elite units of the Wehrmacht . . .

Will the war end in time for the Jews of Budapest to escape the fate of the provincial Jews, and of all the other Jews in occupied Europe?

In early November the machinery of death has started

again. The Red Army nears Budapest. One shelling follows another. The Reich vacillates. The trains are stopped.

But the Nazis continue to concentrate, deport, and kill Jews. "At least, we will have succeeded in this: the final solution," Eichmann is later to say.

And another SS will declare: "If our dream crumbles, this at least will be accomplished."

At night, the Zionists gather and talk about the future. Of Israel—which some of them perhaps will reach.

"For one of us to settle there will be a victory for all of us!"

They harbor no illusions as to their chances of survival. But ideas are stronger than death, and they far outlast life. This, the Nazis will never understand. Only men can be killed.

At night, at the House of Glass, in the other protected houses, in the Jewish houses, and even in the depths of the bunkers and the installation trenches, the young Zionists sing in a low voice the same song, the *Hatikvah:*

As long as there's a Jewish soul that vibrates at the pit of the heart
And as long as our eyes turn toward the East seeking Zion,
As long as our tears flow and the Jordan waters Tiberias,
And the Wall waits for us,
Only with the last of the Jews
Will the last hope disappear . . .

Tomorrow, other rescue operations will be attempted. Pinchas Rosenbaum will put on his Levente uniform, Weiskopf will go out in plain clothes, "Little Skull" as a militiaman. . . . Jews will be snatched from prison, from torture, from deportation. Their sentences will be suspended. Only with the last of the Jews will the last hope disappear.

TWENTY

Raids on the Nazi Prisons

IN THE murderous madness that possesses the Hungarian Nazis in Budapest, what does it matter to have the fragile protection of a neutral safe-conduct or of a flag that pretends to extraterritorialize the building over which it flies? Are the Hazalah leaders right in centralizing in the protected houses —at 29 Vadasz Street, at Red Cross headquarters, or Baross Street, for instance—their information services, their clandestine presses, their modest operational "bases," and their best, their bravest partisans? What about the bunkers and the weapons caches—such as the shelter on Hungaria Boulevard —the secret meeting places where partisans gather for rifle practice in the woods around Budapest? Wouldn't they be safer places?

As it is, upon analysis, the protected houses win out. The

reasoning of the partisans is simple: the "neutrals" represent a screen against the Nazi fury, one that is preferable to no screen at all; the Szalasi government has not been recognized by the neutrals. It is in playing on the future possibility of granting recognition that the consuls and the nunciate have obtained safe-conduct validation from the Arrow Cross. Afterward, realizing that he'd been fooled, Szalasi denounced the agreement. But there is no doubt that he still hopes, even unconsciously, for some unlikely diplomatic recognition, to which he attaches some price. In the face of Hungary's new leaders, the representatives of Sweden, Switzerland, Portugal, and the Vatican are not totally unarmed. For the Jews, almost defenseless, abandoned by the world, it is one of the very few elements of support they have. Perhaps the only one.

Another element—of a geographic nature—has caught their attention. Next door to the House of Glass, at 29 Vadasz Street, is a vacant building, number 31, abandoned, locked, inaccessible from the street: the Hungarian Football Federation. The Zionists have discovered that by establishing some inside access between the two buildings, they will be able to create a kind of extra bunker. The complexity of the House of Glass itself—with its cellars, its courtyards, its many store rooms, its intercom system—offers, in case of siege and even of attack by the enemy, some possibilities of defense, perhaps armed defense. These possibilities are far more numerous than in a simple apartment building, an overexposed command post in the woods, or a bunker in the city that has no emergency exit. Moreover, the use of diplomatic cars flying the Swiss flag, driven by partisans disguised as embassy chauffeurs, could make it possible to maintain permanent liaison with other protected houses and Hazalah centers in the city, which are constantly being moved to keep one step ahead of the raids. Food-supply trucks could also come and go more easily. The analysis will prove correct: till the day of liberation, at the cost of a few alerts and skirmishes, and also, unfortunately, at the cost of victims shot down or kidnapped, the House of Glass, under the false front of neutrality, will play its role as a haven, as the last shelter for the persecuted, as headquarters for the rescue operations. It will become even a kind of symbol, which the unfortunates will cling to in the nothingness of torture and death. One night, a real ghost is to appear there, bloody and exhausted, the miraculous survivor of a mass slaughter on the banks of the Danube. History:

"I was arrested with my daughter. After torturing us—more precisely slashing our backs with razor blades—the Nylas hustled the group, two by two, to the Danube, and began to shoot. I fell into the river. I was only wounded but doubtless I'd have let myself die if, at the last moment, the idea hadn't crossed my mind that in this world of hatred and death, in this pitiless city, a shelter still existed for the Jews—the House of Glass. Almost without thinking, I began to swim through the hail of bullets toward Elisabeth Bridge. It was night. I managed to hoist myself onto a barge with nobody on it. I saw corpses floating by. I waited a moment and then jumped onto the dock. The darkness saved me. Soon after, two partisans on a rescue mission picked me up. I knew where they were taking me."

Commandos regularly leave the House of Glass on ever more difficult missions. Meanwhile, life settles down in this strange Jewish fortress isolated on enemy ground amidst a storm of terror and violence.

Another of the House of Glass refugees, a certain Feigenbaum, "released" from a labor camp thanks to Pinchas Rosenbaum, who managed to provide him with protection papers (Pinchas, for the occasion, took on the identity of a high-ranking Nazi dignitary and succeeded in an audacious bluff against the camp's commanding officer), is astonished to discover a kind of study-and-work community, disciplined, fully active, and oriented toward the future. Material problems are handled by efficient committees, whose authority is unquestioned. Two thousand people—and soon many more—crowd the insufficient space; living conditions, however, are almost bearable.

"One of our greatest fears," Elisabeth Eppler is to say later, "was that the Nazis would shut off the water. We had some reserves, but not enough. Miraculously, in the cellar, there was a hydrant that continued to function up to the very last days of the siege."

Several doctors set up a makeshift hospital; they will often have to treat those wounded by gunshot or shelling, a few cases of scarlet fever and typhoid, but no epidemics. The hospital will never lack medicines, nor blood for transfusions. With every profession, every skill represented at the House of Glass, the trickiest problems find unheard-of solutions. For instance, the problem of building an oven for bread; Gideon, the baker, soon considered it indispensable:

"The architects were unyielding," Elisabeth Eppler recounts; "they clamored for bricks to build their oven with. I suggested to Arthur Weiss, the owner of the House (who still occupied his personal apartment), that we issue an order by telephone to the Sorg brickyard. He remarked that the brickyard's owner was pro-Nazi. But so what? We'll tell him—which was plausible—that the order comes from the Swiss embassy. Lured by profit, he might deliver the merchandise. I was beginning to dial the number when suddenly there was the sound of a tremendous explosion: a shell, or a bomb, had just fallen on the house across the street. The windowpanes flew into pieces, a thick smoke filled Mr. Weiss's office, and I had the feeling that the ceiling was collapsing. A little later, when we surfaced, unharmed, we got a big surprise: the concussion had hurled bricks, torn from the bombed-out house, right into the office. Bricks! Just the right amount to build the bread oven."

The replenishment of food is regularly assured, sometimes at the cost of commando operations as dangerous as rescue missions. The kitchens are committed to the care of a specialist, one Mr. Stern, the evicted owner of a kosher restaurant; at the House of Glass, a great many religious Jews would let themselves starve if there were not rabbinical supervision. Flour, sugar, and condensed milk for the children are scattered in safe caches in the event of a search. The partisans—educated to farming—have planted vegetable gardens in the ruins, following the example of their elders in Warsaw. Some grow potatoes.

Latrines have been dug in the courtyard. Mr. Leo Salzer, owner of a paper mill at Ujpest, in the northern suburbs of the city, is in charge of the toilet paper; when the supply runs low, he doesn't hesitate to make a raid on his own factory, with a three-ton truck and help from the partisans. When they return to the House of Glass, their truck is riddled with bullet holes.

As counterpoint to these exercises in material survival, Hazalah religious, at the House of Glass, pledge themselves to a life of prayer, meditation, and plans for the future. That is what strikes Feigenbaum most when he arrives and is assigned a bed in the attic. As if the reign of the fascist gangs were but an episode, lectures, Hebrew courses, and preparation for life in Israel alternate with prayers and explications of the Law. Small groups form to comment on the Mishnah, or the Gemara.

Choirs rehearse Hebrew songs. As in the Warsaw ghetto, books are very much in demand, and in the black market the price of books rises almost as quickly as the price of food! Professors conduct courses on the history of the Jewish people, sometimes with an emphasis on Titus's siege of Jerusalem, on the destruction of the Temple—tragic episodes that were to provoke the Diaspora. Will the present siege and the new extermination in Europe mark, 19 centuries later, the end of the scattering? The few partisans who have had any experience in Israel are listened to passionately.

What Feigenbaum discovers, in the very heart of Budapest, in the House of Glass, is the life of a kibbutz preparing for the "going up" to Israel, for a peasant life in the Promised Land, for the creation of a Jewish society founded upon the teaching of the Torah. Under the menace of the Nazis—whom they hear passing in the street shouting invectives—the House of Glass residents fervently pursue their apprenticeship of collective and messianic responsibility, directed toward the return to their ancestral land.

On November 8, the sound of Soviet artillery becomes so distinct that partisans who have worked on the front, in the labor brigades, can distinguish the sound of "Stalin's organs," the mortars, the "Katioucha." To all the Jews in Budapest, these rumblings, bearing the promise of liberation, offer reason for hope. But this Red Army advance also stirs up the fury of the Nazis. Alarming news accumulates: regrouping camps have been improvised—in synagogues on Dohany and Rumbach streets, for instance. More than 6,000 Jews have been packed together there, under dreadful conditions. Any move is forbidden them, even the removal of dead bodies. There is talk of their leaving by foot—trains are running only with great difficulty these days on the bombed-out railroads—for an easily imagined destination. Another piece of information plunges the Hazalah leaders into anxiety: the Nylas are said to be preparing the erection of a fence around the "Jewish quarter"—the ghetto—where 100,000 still live in seclusion. Several Zionists who have managed to infiltrate the ranks of Nazi Hungarian youth organizations and attend their meetings confirm the decision. Soon, Budapest's Jewish quarter will be as isolated as was the Warsaw ghetto.

In the face of the desperate operation beginning to take shape, Hazalah decides to intensify its rescues. As many Jews as possible must be snatched from the future ghetto, most of them placed in the protected houses, Schutzpasses distributed, all possible means used to prevent the closing of the trap on those who have survived. They will respond to the increased violence by an increase in the number of rescues.

They work day and night. At the House of Glass, a partisan is assigned control of the list of names; he fills out thousands of certificates—last name, first name, birthdate. He checks to see that photographs and names match and gives the documents to the distribution specialists, who then divide up the completed work among the "messenger" crews. Their mission seems easy: to contact the right person and deliver the certificate; but they have to get the certificate validated by whatever authority is holding their protégé. Very often, this last phase can only be accomplished through a stroke of daring, a desperate maneuver that sometimes goes beyond the point of no return. It is not enough to present the document. To make it work, they have to stick their necks out. How many messengers lost everything in the course of these missions? On this point, no figures exist.

"I saw many of our young people, going out in uniforms of every type, an assortment of documents in their pockets," recalls one of the House of Glass survivors. "When one of them didn't come back, we always hoped he had found shelter in another protected house or in a bunker. We waited for information. Then hope petered out, and we avoided the subject. There were always new volunteers—and so many poor souls needing help out there."

Some partisans "go out" almost daily. There are those,

such as Moshe Weiskopf, alias Horak, who choose to play the neutral diplomat or Red Cross representative. They place their confidence in minute details: a genuine leather briefcase, a brand-new leather coat, well-polished boots. . . . Others, like Emmeric Deutsch, pretend to be employees at the Swiss legation, or, like Zvi Goldfarb, alias Mario Marchesi, Italian worker, stick to borrowed identities and play Nazis in positions of influence. Others still, like Pinchas Rosenbaum, try to mix with the German enemy by resembling him to the last detail. At all times, they must be cautious, without letup. And, in case of failure, accept torture and death.

Few indeed are the Hazalah survivors who have not, at least once, experienced an arrest and torture. Their only comfort lay in the certainty that everything would be done to free them—if they just held on. Inside the Hazalah operation, the rescue of imprisoned comrades is a special one where boldness, ingenuity, and the spirit of sacrifice, rise to an almost incredible pitch.

One night, toward the end of November, while an icy rain falls on the famished city, prostrate, bombed out, the news arrives at the House of Glass that Zidi (Zeinenfeld) has been arrested. He is at the Gestapo headquarters, at the Majestic Hotel. They know he has been caught before being able to deliver his Schutzpasses. Zidi operates in civilian clothes, under the name of Kovacs, a Swiss-legation employee, and he carries a briefcase. Through a contact they cultivate at the Majestic, the partisans learn that Zidi, in very bad condition after a first interrogation, has been transferred to the Nazi-controlled hospital on Wesselenyi Street. Why hadn't they liquidated him? Because the Gestapo wants to gather proofs of a "Zionist conspiracy," and the interrogation specialists, convinced that their prisoner belongs to an organized network, want to put him back in shape in order to get the information from him. It is evident that Zidi won't survive another torture session. He holds on only through the hope of rescue. If this hope doesn't come true very soon, he will commit suicide—if he can.

Till midnight, on Vadasz Street, the Zionists hold a council. And come to the conclusion that the only chance to get Zidi out of hell is to force their way to him. All agree to take the risks; all are volunteers. Finally they select two partisans who have already succeeded in "sorties" as dangerous as the present one and therefore have experience to add to audacity, courage, and the spirit of sacrifice: Pinchas Rosenbaum—from the Misrahi—and Yosi—an agricultural student from the Hashomer Hazair. Departure is set for 3 A.M. The two boys put on SS uniforms, the long, green leather coats of officers; they check their weapons and sneak off into the night in the direction of the hospital.

They have no real, preconceived plan, for they lack items of information. They rely on their luck, and on God's protection. At every intersection, they slow down imperceptibly to reconnoiter. In the cold drizzle, Pest looks like a dead city. In the distance, the battle cannons rumble, and from time to time a pinkish glow tints the sky.

With an assured gait, they draw near their goal as they enter a street as deserted as the others, their last straight stretch. But there is a sound, and it sends chills up their spines: the stomp of boots that seems to echo their own tempo. No doubt is possible, it is a patrol. Two SS walk toward them—long coats, caps with the death's head, shiny boots, and Tommy guns at the ready.

The two partisans maintain their pace. There is no way to avoid the confrontation. Any wrong move, any sudden attempt to flee would betray them. A serious situation, because in the present turmoil, the Nazis—true Nazis—trust neither uniforms nor papers. Even among the SS they have to give an account of themselves with passwords that change several times a day. Pinchas and Yosi don't know the password. Everything will be decided in a second.

Is there a solution? A Hitlerian salute, an outstretched arm, a "*Heil* Hitler" won't save them. Pinchas pauses to steel himself. As for Yosi, his mind is made up. Without giving his comrade time for a word, he empties the entire clip of his Tommy gun on the two SS from a distance of five yards; the sound of the burst fills their ears, but these days, in the city, gunshots no longer wake anyone.

Though they live in the neighborhood of death, death is still an outrage to them. Pinchas is paralyzed for a moment. But Yosi is already busy. The two bodies are stretched out on their backs. A piece of paper is hastily pinned to one of the uniforms: "This is the fate awaiting the filthy Jew who dares to wear the SS uniform." It is a line the two pioneers had read not long ago on two other victims in a street nearby. They seize the identification papers of the real Nazis—and resume their walk. With the same assured gait.

Soon after, they arrive at the hospital gate, guarded by a convalescent Jew. The man is ordered to fetch Zidi! Terrorized, he claims this is beyond his authority; he has to leave it up to his bosses. The two partisans then reveal their identities:

"If I surrender the prisoner to you," the guard groans, "the SS will have me shot . . ."

"We'll take you with us. Get going!"

A short time later, a group of four men—three of them dragging a very weak prisoner—enter Wesselenyi Street. They walk past the two SS corpses without stopping. Direction: the House of Glass, where they arrive without further mishap at about 4:30 A.M. Zidi still has his famous leather attaché case. In their rage—an astonishing detail—the police have neglected to search it. It still contains the hundred blank Schutzpasses. At dawn, messengers will go and distribute them in the ghetto.

Except for those who try to survive in the city under false identities, all the Budapest Jews are now in the ghetto, behind the fence, and this situation is alarming to the Hazalah. They have always advocated scattering, blending, as a weapon against collective slaughter. Now the enemy has succeeded in bunching the mass of survivors—making its task all the easier!

An order is issued to attempt the impossible so that the Jews can be placed under neutral protection—or be disguised. The presses increase their output of documents to meet the demands of the new situation.

But more and more frequently the partisans are arrested while on their missions. Rescue operations are stepped up too. At the Margitkerut military prison in Buda, Zionist commandos, led by Joel Palgi, present themselves in Hungarian police uniforms, with false summonses to appear before the military court presiding at the Hadik barracks. It is a gigantic bluff, but it works. The roll is called in the courtyard. The prisoners are certain that they are being picked to be shot on the banks of the Danube. The partisans manage to throw them hints and to make them understand the situation by mispronouncing their first names; they want to avoid any burst of despair. Among the released prisoners are Zvi (Mario Marchesi) Goldfarb and Neska—who were betrayed, arrested, then tortured for weeks. As soon as they are free, their main concern is to evacuate the Red Cross house on Boron Street: the Nazis know what has been going on there. In the night, the freed prisoners part, each having received an address, a shelter. Some time later, a similar mission is carried out at the Foutca prison. The Zionists have enlisted the services of two real Hungarian policemen, several Nylas, and two Gestapo agents. The operation is expensive; the Waada Zionist movement has lent the funds.

All the partisans, all the leaders, side by side, are now involved in the great rescue enterprise. The Red Army advances on Budapest. The war is coming to a close. But in this ominous November 1944, the threat becomes ever more precise for the last of the Jews, penned up in the ghetto, starving, sick, their nerves stretched to snapping. Between them and a death seldom avoided, often wished for, new, painful experiences, new suffering will arise. The Hazalah pioneers are ready for the final combat. Hanna Szenes, the little paratrooper from Israel, has been shot after a summary trial. Before coming for shelter to the House of Glass—where she stood in line without identifying herself—her mother went to the Margitkerut prison. They gave her her daughter's clothes. In a pocket, she found two pieces of paper. On one was a poem, ending in these words:

> Death is over my head.
> In July, I'll be 23 years old;
> I played a daring game,
> The die is cast . . .
> I've lost.

"She was proud, literally proud to be Jewish," Major Simon, the Hungarian officer commanding the prison, added, without hiding his astonishment.

TWENTY-ONE

Jews in SS Uniforms

IN EARLY November 1944, the hunt for Jews is at its peak in Budapest. The Nazi press—and propaganda—hold them responsible for the disloyalty of Regent Horthy, now an internee in Germany. For Eichmann's men, for the Arrow Cross, this "treason" of the Jews calls for only one sentence: death. Incitements to murder are launched in every newspaper; whoever kills a Jew, posters proclaim, serves the nation! After the spring massacres, the winter massacres.

The existing legislation, already harsh, is no longer considered sufficient. It becomes obvious that able-bodied Jews, commandeered for installation work, are being exterminated little by little. Escapees have witnessed summary executions in the forest. Entire groups disappear, with no trace of them ever to be found. The shooting has resumed, as it had the day after the coup d'état. Protection from the neutrals becomes more and more illusory. Even though those houses that have been turned into fortresses still stand fast, the isolated Jews are more and more treated like outlaws, no matter what documents they brandish. The Nylas have announced that they know false Schutzpasses are in circulation. They also know that many Jews, escapees from the locked ghetto, bury themselves in the Aryan part of the city without any papers or under false IDs. The Hungarians underestimate the number of these covert Jews (they actually number more than 30,000). But they seldom pardon those they discover. The law gives them the right to shoot on sight any Jew whose false ID is "apparent and proved."

Will the survivors stick it out? The Soviet army is approaching. The regular Hungarian troops flow back from the front, with Jewish M.U.S.Z. workers. Desertions abound. For the Nazis, the Jews are potential partisans, ready to lend aid to the Soviet fighters. One more reason to neutralize them, before the first of the inevitable street fighting.

It is all absurdity, delirium, despair. In the face of this situation, however, the Hazalah keep calm.

The "neutral" documents lose their protective value through excessive duplication. Instead of the 7,800 official titles of protection issued by the legations, tens of thousands are in circulation. Lutz and Wallenberg continue their efforts (leaning on the minister of foreign affairs, Baron Kemeny, who still hopes to gain some "recognition" for his criminal government), but they encounter increasing difficulty in dealing with the Nazis. On November 5, Hazalah puts its eleventh-hour plan into practice. The operational groups receive their separate powers. Orders are given them not to let a single contingent of prisoners leave for a regrouping camp or a forced labor camp without attempting, in one way or another, to detain it. And to try again when they fail.

Luckily, intelligence works well. The headquarters on Vadasz Street and the one on Weckerle Street are very quickly informed of all the initiatives of the enemy. For instance, one day, an anonymous, anguished phone call announces that the children's house on Nagyfavaros Street is about to be "evacuated"; there can be no doubt that death awaits the little orphans.

Coça Grunwalt calls the police; the house, he says, is placed under the protection of the Swiss legation (which is true). He gets a dirty laugh for an answer: "Swiss protection or Jewish protection?" And they hang up on him.

Something else must be done. Laci Kepes decides to risk a whopping bluff. Aren't Palgi, Grunwalt, Goldfarb, and other Zionists successful every day with the same ploy? He borrows Grunwalt's leather coat, a briefcase, and gold-rimmed eyeglasses.

"This leather coat," Grunwalt recounts, "was famous at Hazalah. It was a kind of good-luck charm. It had already helped in many rescue missions. But the mission Kepes was setting out on seemed so risky that I thought I'd never see my comrade again, nor my coat. . . ."

Phlegmatic, Kepes climbs into the Red Cross car kept in reserve for such missions—the bullet holes having been more or less camouflaged. Objective: the children's house. A Nylas sentry bars the way. Kepes addresses him with a theatrical display of indignation.

"How dare you penetrate international territory? Go and get the officer in charge!"

Kepes's tone—and his leather coat—produces the desired effect. The sentry comes back with a Hungarian officer. The whole game lies in the first exchange of words. The partisan raises his voice even higher and brandishes the documents.

"I have orders," the officer answers.

"Let me see them!"

The children, lined up in the courtyard, follow the scene with interest, but they are not upset. The youngest of them are two or three years old. They hold hands. Abandoned orphans, herded from camps to houses for months, they are used to long waits, counter orders; starving, they no longer know how to laugh. Their fate has hardened their faces. Kepes decides to play his top card:

"If you and your men don't leave this house immediately, I'll telephone Baron Kemeny (the least hostile to the "neutrals" in the Szalasi government). You'll all be thrown into jail . . ."

Audacity pays: the Arrow Cross men apologize and leave the "protected house." Kepes and the Red Cross chauffeur—another Zionist partisan—make several trips to take the children and the personnel to Vadasz Street. There's always room for one more. Grunwalt's leather coat has a new victory to its credit.

The Hazalah partisans have studied the possibilities offered by hospitals and dispensaries and have decided on using false epidemics as a defensive weapon. The enemy could be kept in check by a contagious disease, and all the more so because the first cases of typhus have been reported in Budapest as early as the beginning of November. A hospital can certainly be used as a shelter, in the same way as the protected houses and bunkers.

One day, by chance, a young Jew comes to the Weckerle Street Red Cross in the uniform of a medical-corps cadet; that is when they decide to create a hospital-shelter in the city. After a study of the situation with Drs. Breslauer and Roth, Coça Grunwalt becomes the head of a strange medical-commando unit assigned to set up a phony Nylas establishment where Jews, disguised as contagiously ill Nazis, would be hidden. The cadet knew everything there was to know about how a medical corps worked; he had been in one for two years under a false identity. He had noted the weaknesses and defects of the system. He believed that there was a good chance of success, especially if someone offered to create a hospital for the "Hungarist Legion," a military outfit the Germans held in esteem.

Disguised as Nylas, with papers from the 32nd section, led by their Hungarist Legion doctors, the partisans decide to go to City Hall and request an audience with Nidossy, chief of the Legion, a high dignitary in the Hungarian Nazi Party, and head of the health department in Budapest. (Before the war, Nidossy was a pedicurist in a fashionable bath house in Buda!) His command post now is located in the basement of City Hall; the partisans reach it after a long trudge underground. At every checkpoint, Nylas sentries stop the partisans, their Tommy guns at the ready. The cadet's uniform and his energetic salutes clear the way at every turn. Even today, Coça Grunwalt can't recall this astonishing expedition without breaking into a sweat.

At the door of the health chief's office, a Nylas officer stands guard. They have to inveigle their way into the chief's office. Of course the idea that this group which has reached the very core of the fortress could be composed of Jews doesn't even occur to him. As expected, once more the almost absurd boldness of the operation diverts suspicion.

Nidossy listens to their request; in the present state of the situation—Budapest is practically under siege—and taking into account the difficulties of running the ever scarcer ambulances and the crowding of the main hospitals, the partisans' project seems to interest him. He insists that the Hungarist Legion receive priority in the establishment—this is "accepted" by the partisans—and, while paying homage to the patriotism that inspires these young Nylas, he signs the papers the cadet presents to him. What is even better—

Nidossy gives the Zionists a special-mission warrant—duly stamped—enabling them to submit all the necessary requisitions! And he wishes them good luck.

That day, the phony Nylas, led by Grunwalt, install their dispensary in the basements of Cinema City, where it will operate throughout the siege. Its front is a treatment center for a few Legion members—wounded or ill—while in wards labeled "seriously contagious" numerous Jews are hospitalized, some of them seriously wounded or ill. The partisans also open an emergency exit, foreseeing a possible inspection—which is never to occur.

Arrests go on. Caught in the street, or simply kidnapped at home, the Jews are assembled either in the Kissok Stadium or in the Buda brickyard where detention conditions are appalling. There are very few able-bodied men—most of them work at military installations—and the regrouping places are largely populated by women, the aged, the sick, the disabled, and children. Through the contacts they keep up among the Nylas, the partisans know that Solymossy, the chief of the Hungarian Nazi police, and Ferenczy, the policeman who wants to be forgiven his onetime weakness for Horthy, are bringing pressure on the Germans to resume the deportations, without jeopardizing their other plans for massacre.

The trains are no longer running. In mid-November the bombings by Allied aviation and the Red Army are intensified. The tracks are unusable (the last trains crossing the border north carried condemned Jews). At Hazalah, some feel that, under these conditions, the Jews concentrated in the old Buda brickyard are safe from deportation. They are wrong. On November 14 the news arrived at Vadasz Street and the other protected houses: the Hungarians and the Germans are deporting the Jews—on foot!

At first, it seems unbelievable. How can they make these women, these old people, these sick, underfed children walk all the way to the border—and beyond—and through the cold that is getting worse? The enterprise would not have seemed feasible even with able-bodied men.

Nevertheless, the news is confirmed: columns of marchers are being formed at the brickyard, and the poor victims, under the eyes of the police, Nylas, and members of the Gestapo, are being herded onto the road. Official destination: the Austrian border—150 miles away! Other columns, it is learned, are to leave from Kissok football stadium. The Hungarian Jews are going to their death on foot.

In the city, more and more Jews are being turned in. Hanni Lichtmann, a young Jew from Slovakia, has taken cover in a Christian house, at 33 Nagyatadi Szabo Street. Turned in, she's arrested by the Nylas but manages to escape from the police station. With no papers, she is lost. She decides to go back home, with the idea that she can get there faster than the police; she has a set of false documents cached away in the apartment. But her calculations prove wrong. The police get there first; they have seized the papers, and they are waiting for her. Once more, she is roughed up and arrested:

"This time you won't get away from us, you filthy Jew!"

The Nylas, however, go by a different route this time, and they end up on Vadasz Street. They are partisans, and it is one more rescue to the credit of Pinchas Rosenbaum's commandos. Learning of the arrest—and the girl's escape—they profit from their extreme mobility and the swiftness of their actions, accomplishing the saving of one more life.

But the accumulation of refugees in the protected houses begins to raise serious problems of supply and organization. They are able to handle them for the moment, but the future looks bleak.

There are moments of depression on Vadasz Street. But

they do not last. The religious Zionists, especially, make sure that hope is constantly kept alive. Those who have lost heart are taken in hand, integrated into a group. They talk to them of Israel, of a future of justice and happiness, and of God. Even in the worst holocaust, the young say, there is the budding idea of renewal. They evoke the destruction of the Temple of Jerusalem, which gave birth to the propagation of the Talmudic spirit, to this astounding awakening of faith—a faith of which the young religious partisans are the trustees. Are they not dedicating themselves to this cause? Truly, the courage they display, their altruism, represent a tremendous lesson in hope. Are they not refusing the money Jews offered them in exchange for false documents? Are they not risking their lives daily to save total strangers, simply because they are Jews and are being persecuted?

Such are their faith, their calm, and their unshakable confidence that they are able to wipe out the reality. At the House of Glass, their influence grows stronger. Inspired by their example, Weiss, the old landlord will go to the Hungarian officers' club to enjoy his after-dinner drink, in defiance of the Nylas. He will continue to go up to the last days of the siege, in the middle of the battle, while bullets whiz past him. He will not wear the Star of David, trusting in his own star.

TWENTY-TWO

The Death March

ON NOVEMBER 16, a group of SS officers, including generals and the Auschwitz commandant, Höss, arrive at the Majestic by car from Vienna and express their surprise: on their way they have passed pitiful groups of marchers flanked by soldiers and gendarmes. The dying and the dead of all ages dotted the route. The sight revolted them, not for its cruelty but because it was the kind of thing that could awaken the pity of the Hungarian people in favor of the deported Jews and attract the attention of the neutral countries. Moreover, hasn't Himmler just ordered that the death factories be dismantled and an end put to mass extermination?

Eichmann is on assignment; the orders for deportation by foot are canceled. But Eichmann returns to Budapest on the 21st and puts them back into effect, asserting that he is acting under Hitler's personal directives.

The death march! Eichmann's trial later brings to light unknown, or little-known, elements about the circumstances under which the deportations were ordered, discussed, suspended, resumed. We know in particular that the operation reflected the conflict existing between two cliques of the Gestapo—one Schellenberg's, the other Kaltenbrunner's. The marches went on for almost five weeks—from early November to December 10. Forty thousand men, women, old people, and children took part. Nearly 10,000 of them died.

Eichmann, ignoring the recommendations of Himmler, pretended to "concentrate" 70,000 Hungarian Jews, survivors of previous actions, at the Austro-Hungarian border for the purpose of building a last line of defense. At Hazalah no one believed that the "defense line" would be anything other than a means of extermination. Death was at the end of the journey, as with all the other "actions."

From the first departures, Hazalah operations mounted to help on the journey the unfortunate men and women they had not been able to save or hide earlier.

The Zionists had seen many terrible things, but what they now discovered surpassed in horror anything they could have imagined. The marches were from 15 to 20 miles a day, sometimes without food, in freezing cold. There were even, between Gönyü and Dunaszeg for instance, marches as long as 25 miles. Exhausted, sick, the marchers slept on the bare ground in the ditches along the Budapest-Vienna highway. The stragglers, or those too weak to keep up, were shot where they were by the Nylas or the Arrow Cross. The death rattles of children were heard in the ditches. Women suffering miscarriages offered a bloody spectacle to the jeering soldiers. The old begged to be finished off and got only a snicker in return. Some went mad.

For sport, the Nylas sometimes organized mock executions; they forced the marchers to dig a common grave. They lined them up at the edge, and then, laughing uproariously, dismissed them. Sometimes they would conduct a search. Any Jew found with money was undressed, then whipped to death in front of his horrified companions. Sometimes the condemned man was stripped naked and, at nightfall, immersed in a barrel or doused with water. His torturers would wait until he turned into a block of ice and had the deportees file past him, or had him carried around among them.

As the Nazi leaders had feared, the very excesses of the sufferings endured by the deportees sometimes attracted the sympathies of the peasants, however little inclined they were to feel any compassion or solidarity toward the Jews. One did see—something that happened very seldom in Hungary—women bringing water or even bread to the condemned. A few humane gestures brought the horrible death march some glimmer of light. It was again for the partisans the occasion for incredible rescue missions. A survivor recalls:

"We were arrested in the Jewish house at 36 Czaky Street, where 20 families were packed together. On November 9, very early in the morning, soldiers invaded the courtyard, wearing the red brassards with a green arrow cross in a white circle. Everyone was ordered to come down. We had Schutzpasses that the partisans had managed to get to us several days before, but the soldiers declared them void and tore them up.

" 'All the Jews have become Swiss or Hungarian protégés,' said an officer, laughing. 'We know very well who makes these papers.'

"A 50-year-old man who protested had his forehead opened by the butt of a rifle. Blinded by the blood, he followed our group which the Nylas, shouting, led toward Rudolf Quay, along the Danube. Many thought they would be shot on the quay; children cried but, as a whole, the Jews submitted to their fate with great dignity. At one moment, two young men in leather coats, with Nylas brassards, walked past the soldiers. They exchanged Nazi salutes.

" 'More Jewish riff-raff!' one of them said. 'Wipe out these vermin!' The other one burst out laughing. But when they got up to us, the boy who had just spoken told us quickly, in a low voice, 'Don't lose faith, the Halutzim are watching over you.'

"There were only three or four of us who heard what he said, in Yiddish, but we passed it on. A little hope returned.

"On Rudolf Quay, there were already a number of Jews—for the most part women, old people, and children, all of them undressed. The Nylas seemed to hesitate. Finally, an order was shouted: to the brickyard!

"There, a hopeless spectacle awaited us; thousands of famished people, sick and moaning, were jammed into the sheds and the yards. A nauseating stink hung in the air. Old people were dying on the bare ground. A friend I ran into told me, 'It's hell. Nothing to eat, nothing to drink. Escape is impossible. Not one contact with the outside.'

"In fact, two purported envoys from the Swiss legation, who the day before had got into the brickyard, claiming the release of the 'protected,' had simply been put under arrest. They were Jews claiming to be Swiss. Unmasked by an informer, they were tortured; their moanings could be heard all night. In the morning, their broken bodies were exposed in the yard by the Nylas: their eyes were pierced out, their genitals yanked off; they had been practically skinned alive. One of them, however, was still breathing. He had the strength to whisper, 'Courage!'

"Contact nil, escape impossible—and no food for two days. At the Buda brickyard, inmates threw themselves against the walls, screaming. Then, one morning, an order was shouted in the yard for everyone to form ranks. In a frenzy, the Nylas beat to death whoever was unable to stand up straight. Some chose this painful way to commit suicide. The procession then started out.

"The pace set by the Nylas was fast and, after a mile or two, marchers began to fall and were unable to get up. They were shot where they lay. In the evening, Hungarian police arrived by truck to relieve the Nylas. I had decided to fight to the last ounce of strength in me. But many of those who walked with me flagged and let themselves fall without a word. You conserved the tiniest spark of energy; you didn't even say 'farewell.' You ignored the children when they asked, 'Where are we going? When will we get there? I'd like to stop, my feet hurt. . . . Are we going to eat soon, or sleep?'

"The official destination, which the Nylas had announced when we set out, was Vienna, but no one really believed we'd reach the Austrian capital. We had the feeling that this march would end in an extermination camp or even with us facing machine guns out in the country. However, there were a few of us who fought back.

"No sooner had we departed, in fact, than a rumor went the rounds, which the encounter with the phony Nylas, near Rudolf Quay, made plausible: there were partisans around us, hidden among the real Nylas. They could not disclose themselves, but they were there, watching over us.

"It was true. During the night, young Zionists would succeed, on their hands and knees, in getting in among the groups of marchers asleep under the stars, despite the freezing cold (warm clothing was very scarce and many even had no coats). Armed and dressed as Hungarian soldiers, they brought us clothes, shoes, water, sometimes a little bread with margarine—and most of all words of encouragement:

" 'In Budapest a rescue operation is being prepared on a

grand scale. You must hold on till the border. Hazalah is looking out for you.'

" 'Hold on? But how? Most of us are weak, everybody has a fever, dysentery is everywhere.'

" 'To hold on, that's the whole thing.'

"The luckiest of the marchers were those who found a shelter—a stable, a barn—to spend the night in. Sometimes the partisans would say, 'Neutral-country diplomats are negotiating with the Hungarian Nazis and with the police. You'll be taken back to Budapest, in trucks.' And they melted into the night.

"In fact, one morning, I saw an American car with a foreign flag—a Studebaker—coming in the direction of our column. Someone told me it was a Swedish diplomat who took great pains to snatch innocents from death. He would go so far as to threaten the police and the Nylas! And soon the rumor went around that the diplomat had brought Jews back under Swedish 'protection,' and that he would return to pick up others.

"The border, according to the best informed among us, was 120 miles away. Would we be rescued before reaching it? Those who were still in satisfactory physical condition had no other hope. Anguished, we searched for the slightest sign of encouragement."

Actually, the difficulties were sometimes becoming insurmountable for the Hazalah rescuers. The nearness of defeat—news from the front was disastrous and the arrival of the Red Army was expected momentarily—multiplied tenfold, the cruelty and the brutality of the Nazi executions. It was as if they were heaping vengeance in advance upon the innocent Jews for the misfortunes that lay in wait for them. At Gönyü, in spite of the personal support the ardent Wallenberg had lent to it, an operation resulted in failure.

A column of marchers had just reached the city. To cross the Danube, the Jews had been put onto rafts. It was uncertain whether they were to be landed on the other bank or drowned. The partisans launched a last-ditch rescue attempt—with a "neutral" car, a fake Swedish crew, and false diplomatic papers. But the police were not fooled. The mooring lines were let go . . . and the rafts carried off by the current.

The partisans never let themselves become disheartened; when intimidation failed—and providing they had succeeded in saving their own lives, which was not always the case—they resorted to bribery. Jews were released through bottles of rum and packs of cigarettes furnished by the legations. Such exchanges were generally carried out at night:

"Take ten," said a policeman. "So many Jews die we don't even bother to take a roll call. . . ." In this manner they saved the mother of Hanna Szenes, the little Israeli paratrooper. She was then taken in by peasants, at the end of a 60-mile ordeal.

In certain cases, the Zionists even succeeded in tending the sick on the side of the road, in delivering babies for women who had arrived at full term. All the Budapest Jews who still enjoyed some measure of freedom, or who benefited from some cover, helped them. Along the roads, Moshe Krausz—the Jewish Agency representative—Dr. Breslauer, Dr. Kopner, and other phony neutral diplomats were seen to risk their lives in desperate operations that put them in direct contact with the Nazis and that left them, in case of failure, no way out. Many Jews were thus brought back home to Budapest; some even were snatched two or three times from the death procession (arrested again, they would be again thrown onto the road, and again rescued)!

The cold worsened; food rations were never more than a bit of bread and, on good days, a spoonful of cold soup, with a little fat floating on it. An ineffable sadness rose from the ranks of the unfortunate who dragged on toward death, their eyes lowered to the asphalt of the road, where there were mysterious shapes of snow and ice.

"The sight was so heartbreaking," relates Dr. Alexandre Ungar, leader of some of Hazalah's boldest missions "that we threw ourselves into action without taking time to think. We felt we had no right to think. For life itself stood to lose all meaning."

Dr. Ungar, a dentist, president of the Misrahi in the department of Budapest, had taken extreme care to transform himself convincingly into a diplomat just out of Switzerland. He had rented at great cost a car covered with Swiss flags. A partisan, with a badge on his cap, worked as his chauffeur, another as his secretary. For a while, he was even escorted by a true Hungarian officer—who had demanded 100,000 *pengos* (about $300) in exchange for his protection. The crew traveled the main and secondary roads between Budapest and the border with a supply of Swiss protection passports hidden under the rear seat, stamped and signed but without names or photographs. At each stop, under some pretext the phony Swiss would approach the marchers and ask them for identity photos. Many Jews had kept their Hungarian papers. At night, off to the side, the documents were put together and redistributed to the appropriate persons. Then Dr. Ungar would go up to the Hungarian officer in charge and authoritatively demand those protected by "his" legation. Thus the team saved dozens of condemned persons—at great personal risk, for nothing actually prevented a police officer or a Nazi chief from seizing the "Swiss diplomat" and shooting him on the spot. For that happened many times; spurious diplomats, their cover exposed by a physical check—or turned in by a traitor—were tortured and executed in front of those they attempted to save.

Dr. Ungar often flirted with tragedy, as did all those who followed the death march. At Hegyeshalom, a border town where the deportees were supposed to be turned over to the Germans, he was having a discussion with a police officer, a colonel, invoking as usual the Geneva Convention, international law, Swiss-Hungarian accords, and even the possibility of later protection for "good" policemen. He didn't know that two soldiers had been ordered to search his car. The colonel, wary and inscrutable, awaited their report. By chance, that day, the rescue team was not carrying weapons. The blank protection passports, the rubber stamps, did not look suspect to the soldiers. The discussion went on . . . and a few more deportees were saved, *in extremis*.

On December 8, while the death march is still in progress, Raoul Wallenberg, in his Pest residence, writes a note on the latest events. Its essentials are:

> In the last few weeks, the situation of the Hungarian Jews has become untenable. It seems that 40,000 of them—15,000 men from the M.U.S.Z. and 25,000 arrested in their homes—have been deported by foot in the direction of Austria. The walk is 150 miles long. The low temperatures, the rain and the snow, have made this march inhuman. The deportees have no protection from the elements; they have no shelters for sleeping. Most of them get food only every other day. The dead are numerous along the road, especially among the old, women, and children. The undersigned has seen seven dead bodies while going through Moson-Magyarovar. He had seen the same number the previous night. The secretary of the Portuguese legation has counted 42 corpses, and the vice-premier has admitted to having seen two abandoned corpses. The marchers who are unable to keep up with the procession are shot. We went all the way to the border: Eichmann, the SS Sonderkommando chief, was there to welcome the deportees with beatings and all kinds of mistreatment, before promising them forced labor on the military installations.

The partisans who "work" on the roads even manage to shoot more than 400 yards of film, capturing dreadful scenes on it. This film, brought back to Budapest, is shown to the apostolic nuncio. Overwhelmed, he gives his authorization to take Vatican safe-conducts, blank ones, and implicitly approves the counterfeiting. The "Swiss diplomats" instantaneously transform themselves, just as implausibly, into "envoys from the Vatican." Several partisans don cassocks. Girls even dress as nuns to distribute food and medicine to the marchers.

Suddenly the departures appear to have stopped. Of course, at Hazalah, they do not know that the SS is divided on how to proceed with the extermination program and that the suspension of deportations is the result of these disagreements. The partisans make use of this respite to reorganize their intelligence networks among the Nylas, and their messenger networks, which have suffered heavy losses.

But Eichmann soon succeeds in reimposing his ideas, and the deportations resume. The cold is severe on the road where the unfortunates find themselves again under the threat of whips and Tommy guns. It is early December, and the progress of the Red Army marks time. The whole region between Pest and Debreczen is occupied, but the front seems stabilized. The Nazis, naturally, cry victory. And the threat weighs even more heavily on the Jews who remain in Budapest, in the "small ghetto" of the fifth district, called international because it is full of protected houses, and in the ominous "big ghetto" around the synagogue. The partisans must operate on the roads, but also in the city, where bands of deserters, looters, and young Nazis at the last minute enrolled in the Hynyadi division, called the "armored fist," are now on the prowl, completely out of control. The Hynyadi's eleventh-hour weapon, intended for attacks on Soviet tanks, is a kind of crude one-shot bazooka. The reward for each Russian tank destroyed is two and a half acres of land—after the war. But usually, the volunteers—unleashed killers of every stripe—do not survive their hopeless deeds.

What the young Hazalah partisans will have to face in the last days of the battle is terror and madness.

TWENTY-THREE

The Encircled Ghetto

IN EARLY December, what was called the Jewish quarter, bordered by the streets around the three main synagogues, becomes once and for all "the ghetto"—as in Warsaw. A fence of wooden boards is put up around the buildings and empty lots, across intersections, blocking one exit after the other. The Jews anxiously follow the erection of this fence by the Arrow Cross, the police, and the soldiers. The air raids and the shellings often interrupt the work. But, in a week, the separate crews make the junction: the fence is in place. Only four passages are provided, and from the first day on they are closely guarded; these are at the intersections of Karoly Boulevard and Wesselenyi Street, Nagyatadi Szabor Street and Wesselenyi Street, Rackoczi Avenue and Nagydiofa Street, and Kiraly and Kisdiofa streets. It does not take long for the partisans, disguised as Nylas or as Hungarian officials, to draw a detailed map of the "wall" and its passages. They immediately take account of what means they have for getting in and out of the ghetto, past the Hungarian and SS surveillance. It is clear that Hazalah action, already very strong on the roads between Budapest and the border, will have to be intensified inside the Jewish quarter, now isolated from the world. For those in this trap are condemned to be wiped out. Hasn't Minister Kovartz officially asked, in a cabinet session, for the total extermination of the Budapest Jews?

"Any survivor," he declared, "would be a witness against us."

The building of the fence is of course the beginning of this liquidation project. Besides, death is already at work; the partisans have noted that inside the ghetto the conditions of survival become more problematical every day. Along with famine, epidemics of typhus, typhoid, diphtheria, develop. Dozens of cases are reported. Dysentery spreads. The cold, which gets worse, lessens resistance. In the morning dead bodies are picked up in the streets, as in Warsaw. There is no more food, milk, or medication to be found. There is no more electric power. Water is cut off. Nazi peddlers demand huge sums for a few cubes of sugar, or a handful of rice or flour. Partisans, on missions in the ghetto, succeed in neutralizing some of these peddlers—but others resume their trade. There are groups of German Nazis who mix with them because of rumors that Jews in the ghetto are paying very high prices for food, in gold or in dollars. The rumors are not true, of course.

The one thing the Jews in the ghetto share with the rest of Budapest is the risk of air raids. When they do occur, victims are more numerous in the Jewish sector than elsewhere because they haven't enough shelters, the cellars being full of refugees. Of course there is no fire-fighting system, no first aid. The very few doctors are always over their heads in work. They perform miracles, operating by candlelight, but their means are pitiful. Many among them will commit suicide out of despair.

After every shelling, the scene is frightful. The sick and the wounded die right out in the street. Children wander about, crying, looking for their parents, begging for food. From the first day of the cordoning off, the partisans who get into the ghetto, either through one of the gates, disguised as Nylas, or through the sewers, consider it of primary importance to restore some discipline. The great danger is that morale will collapse, the morale of those entrapped.

The first concern of the partisans is to organize an equitable sharing of the scarce food. Two centers of food distribution are in operation, one on Sip Street, the other—which is kosher—on Wesselenyi Street. But the rations—a few vegetables and a little gruel—become ever more meager. Partisans manage to introduce some food into the ghetto at considerable risk. They also, in one way or another, perform emergency evacuations, in the form of phony arrests.

Moshe Weiskopf, under his usual identity as Horak, a Red Cross employee, enters the ghetto many times a day at the wheel of a truck loaded with provisions. Through gifts of great value in this period of shortage, he has bought the friendship of some of the Hungarian guards. When he leaves they simply check his papers, without searching the cab or lifting the tarp. In this way, Horak removes from the ghetto dozens of adults and children, who find refuge at the Weckerle Street Red Cross, at the House of Glass, in the protected children's houses, or in the "bunkers."

Pinchas Rosenbaum too gains entry to the ghetto. He has managed to infiltrate a Nylas contingent and attends their sinister councils of war. There he learns, one evening, that 12 nuns of the order of Our Lady of Zion, accused of giving aid to the Jews, are threatened with arrest. He manages to inform the Vadasz Street specialists, and the nuns get false IDs that will enable them to take flight and escape the police. Pinchas also learns of other plans of action—for example, when the Nylas increase the punitive "raids"—in other words, looting—in the ghetto. On several occasions, at the head of a small group, Pinchas outstrips the Nazis, makes the arrests, and leads the rescued to the House of Glass. Such operations are daily occurrences in December, although they become ever riskier.

"During one of them," Pauli recalls, "a very weak and skinny mother stumbled as she carried a little child. Six comrades and I had decided to take these unfortunates out of the ghetto under the pretext of liquidating them on the banks of the Danube. It was dusk. It was impossible to make the Jews we were taking with us know who we were, and their anguish was terrible—even more so because, to divert suspicion, we insulted them, pushed them around, and threatened them with our guns.

"If I live a hundred years, I'll never forget the look of that young mother when I held out my arms to take her child from her. 'No!' she said, and her own arms wrapped around the sick, whimpering little thing. I saw madness in her eyes."

The Russians are at the gates of Budapest, now almost completely under siege. From December 8 on, the city is being attacked on three sides. On the 11th the Red Army occupies Vac, a key position on the Danube. The fury of the exterminators mounts; gangs of drunks on the loose enter the ghetto, shouting; under the pretense of making searches, they pillage the Jewish houses and kill "for the fun of it." Hazalah messengers go to warn the threatened Jews; girls disguised as boys occasionally take their turns. The "arrest commandos" are constantly on the move. The hideouts and protected houses are overcrowded. However, to the end, room will be found for the new arrivals; on Vadasz Street, more than 700 refugees are jammed into the supplementary bunker in the Football Federation. They are also jammed into the Red Cross house on Weckerle Street. The test is all the more severe in that rescue raids and commando operations must continue to be organized, based upon reliable information. To discourage the enemy, to confound him, and to neutralize in advance all liquidation operations, the Hazalah leaders, knowing that this is the last phase of a nearly desperate fight, try to vary their methods, to multiply their disguises, and to diversify their objectives. The most active of the partisans never go out twice in the same day in the same disguise. They exchange uniforms, weapons, and papers. They invent units that never existed, uniforms never seen before. Emmeric Deutsch is successively a Red Cross official, militia leader, and neutral legation employee. Pinchas Rosenbaum is a Levente, a Gestapo member, a Nazi dignitary, and a Hungarian officer. For this last transformation, he sports a green hat with a plume and introduces himself as Lukacs.

From all sides, anguished appeals reach Hazalah. The proximity of the Red Army, which is making a pincers move around the city, the news from the Western front, and where the Allies are cutting the last of the Axis divisions to ribbons, and rumors of capitulation rouse the fury of the Hungarian Nazis; every Jew caught outside the ghetto is shot on sight. Others are ambushed, among them one of the most efficient organizers of the Zionist resistance, Otto Komoly. In the ghetto, gangs of policemen and looters multiply the raids and mass slaughter at random. The same uncertainty weighs on the few protected enclaves—neutral nations' houses, with their pitiful flags unfurled.

One morning, a message warns that the Nylas are preparing a raid against the children's house on Michel Munkacsy Street. Immediately, at the Red Cross, a phony Nazi commando unit is organized. Weiskopf-Horak takes command of it. But the partisans get there too late. The raid has taken place; several instructors are wounded; one of them is dead. Everyone else, adults and children, has been taken away by the Nazis. Four little forgotten Jews, five or six years old, wander about in a daze. Mimich, the Hazalah photographer, takes some shots. The partisans have brought cheese with them; they distribute it to the survivors. What is to be done? They decide to take them to the Red Cross house on Benczur Street, one of the Hazalah shelters, where there is a doctor. The shattered children are part of the pitiable procession. They are saved, Weiskopf thinks—but for how long?

On December 3, another crisis for the partisans to deal with: the Nylas are proceeding with the evacuation of the Columbus Street camp. Such a move has been feared for some time. The camp itself is next to the Institute for the Deaf and Dumb. More than 3,000 Jews are crowded there under hideous conditions. Some escapees from the M.U.S.Z. are hidden among them. Hazalah partisans are on the spot, and they possess a small supply of arms. When they realize that the camp and the Institute are surrounded, that they are done for, they receive permission to open fire. It is truly a desperate situation, as has been clear for a long time.

The Nylas are not used to such resistance; the first salvo kills and wounds many in their ranks. They retreat and, as they did at Telecki Square, encircle the whole block. The fight goes on around the central building. The partisans, determined to get as high a price for their lives as they can, resist to the death. There is not a single survivor among the combatants. With all resistance wiped out, the anger of the Nylas is unleashed. They shoot women and children without discrimination, even some of the deaf-mutes who walk up to them, bewildered. The partisans who arrive as reinforcements, in ambulances with Nazi emblems, can do nothing but look on at the massacre. The Nylas do not even let the police approach. In the evening, under a freezing rain, the survivors are taken to Kissok Stadium or to Nylas stations, especially the one on Telecki Square. The fate of the Columbus camp detainees about to be deported or executed gives rise to a number of moves; all the Zionist leaders who are still free—André Biss, Moshe Krausz, and Dr. Siegfried Roth among them—do their best to obtain their release, but in vain.

However, the partisans succeed in snatching some women from the Nylas. Disguised as Nazis, Weiskopf, Rosenbaum, and Salomon having got hold of a horse and carriage, "requisition" several prisoners under the vague pretext of needing help to haul bread. They repeat this quaint maneuver for several days. In the morning, they return no one; to the Nazis, they limit their explanation to, "The Jewish scum didn't want to work! We liquidated them on the banks of the Danube."

Of course, the Nylas eventually think this extermination zeal strange, surpassing as it does their own. On the fourth day, the Zionists are greeted by a wily Hungarian woman guard, Ilona Szöke: "You have to haul bread and bacon? We'll take care of it."

She adds that the night before, the Nylas on duty took charge themselves of punishing the Jews who refused to work and, punctuating her words with a smile, had "a tendency to escape." She opens a door into a bathroom. Bodies of women are piled up, bloody, disjointed, eyes wide, faces twisted by torture. . . . Some of them are still breathing.

"Let us have the bread and bacon," the policewoman says quietly.

Weiskopf even today wonders how, in the uniform he was wearing, he was able to keep his self-control.

"Good work, comrade," he said, "we couldn't have done better!"

After the war, Weiskopf was a prosecution witness at the

trial of the guard Ilona Szöke. She was sentenced to ten years in prison. She fainted when she heard the verdict.

The murderous madness has no end, no limit. The Nazis kill for pleasure; they torture from lack of anything better to do. Sometimes they go so far as to kill each other. Some Nylas, becoming suspicious of the behavior of a German SS, force him to take off his pants; the man is circumcised (as a result of an illness, he protests), and they prepare to execute him despite his protests. The SS manages to get a message out to his comrades, however. They arrive in time to free him and, without flinching, massacre every Arrow Cross on the spot, because every one of them is considered guilty of an unforgivable error.

In all the absurdity and madness that encircles them, the partisans try to keep their heads. From all available signs, the enemy is losing control of his own actions. He is like a cornered animal, all the more dangerous for being the more vulnerable. But in the midst of such a frightful massacre, keeping oneself in hand verges on heroism.

The partisans' sorties are stepped up. But, unfortunately, so are the arrests. Armed partisans, having exhausted all their resources, seek death in ultimate combat, according to the guidelines of their movement: M.U.S.Z. escapees, who had succeeded in infiltrating a special police detachment (Pronay), are betrayed and arrested; they are hanged secretly in Margrit Boulevard prison (where Hanna Szenes was shot). Others disappear in suicide missions, the memories of which have not been preserved. On December 13, during a big Nylas rally at the City Theater, renamed the House of Hungarian Culture under the actual chairmanship of General Beregffy, minister of war, a bomb explodes in a box, interrupting the speech of Major Gera. Revolvers drawn, the Nylas marshals try to restore order, when a second explosion shakes the hall. The militants rush toward the exits. Outside, the Hungarians who follow the speech over the loudspeakers that are hung from the trees in Tisza-Kalman Square witness the panic. A rumor quickly spreads: "The Jews did it!"

Enraged, the Nylas marshals engage in savage repression. Their fury fanned to its utmost, they arrest every suspect, going to the depths of the prisons to pick up prisoners whose sentences have not been set. One of them, Hermann Mendel, a 19-year-old partisan from a far-left group, is singled out, without proof, as the perpetrator. A grenade has been found on him. Koltay, assistant to the chief of the Hungarian Gestapo, himself takes charge of the "interrogation." The partisan dies, without talking. In its issue of December 19, the *National Guardian,* the Arrow Cross publication, reveals what is behind the "act of terrorism at the City Theater": "The murderer was the 'Talmudist Jew' Hermann Mendel, born in Safad, Palestine, of Rumanian nationality.' "

The rest of the article is a rehash of the usual accusations dragged out against the Jews: ritual murder, black marketeering, links with occult powers, and so on. The author adds that the executed Mendel had, before dying, turned in all the members of his "network of religious terrorism. Arrested, these malefactors won't have long to wait [after their trial] to pay for their crimes . . ."

This threat, however, fails to convince the Nylas. On December 31, Nazi police break into the House of Glass, under the pretext of gaining information about the Zionists "responsible for the December 13 attempt." They suspect they are hiding in a protected house.

In the quarantined enclave that the ghetto has become, the situation is disastrous. Famine has settled in; the partisans find it more and more difficult to bring in food and medication. Rosenbaum, Deutsch, Weiskopf-Horak, Pil, Efra, Rafi, Grunwalt, and dozens of others have their eye out for any chink in the wall—a wall of wood and hate—that isolates the Jewish quarter. Desperately, they seek to save lives, because

Budapest is now almost totally encircled—and the Red Army's liberation of the city is expected. No one anticipates a long siege. Except the Nazis.

To see the ghetto without heat, without electricity, prey to famine and illness, and in a misery ceaselessly feeding upon itself, is hardly bearable. However, when they return to one of the houses of the international ghetto, where the threat is less acute, the partisans' spirits revive.

At the House of Glass, where 20 are jammed into a room, 50 to a stairway, they continue to celebrate the religious rites, as though life is following its normal course. In the attic, young Orthodox partisans observe the religious rules. Common prayers are said regularly, morning and evening. The sacred scrolls are read three times a week, the teaching of the Talmud is kept up.

In the morning, pious youngsters take off their prayer shawls, kiss the phylacteries, and then turn themselves into Hungarian militia, into Arrow Cross, into SS. They also have to change their expressions, their faces, to go from prayer to insult. For their sole chance of success is to resemble their executioners.

Those who return—unfortunately not all—plunge back into study and meditation and the rituals, the symbolism of which acts as solace. The feast of Hanukkah (the Feast of Lights) in December commemorates the victory of the Maccabees (175 years before the Christian era) over the troops of Antiochus Epiphanes. The historical circumstances evoke the redolent sadness of the present. Didn't Antiochus, mad despot and exterminator, profane the Temple, forbid the practice of the Law, impose false idols upon the Jews? Wasn't he responsible for the revolt that erupted against him—an all-powerful enemy with organized forces at his disposal (including combat elephants) and numbers a thousand times superior? And wasn't this on the part of the Jewish people a desperate fight against death? And a miraculous victory?

The similarity can only deepen the feelings of the Zionists. In the improvised candlesticks, most of the time just simple pieces of wood, they light one candle the first day, two the second—up to eight the eighth day (the time of the miracle granted by God to make the reserve of consecrated oil last and to keep the flame in the Temple from being extinguished). Their prayers take on a singular resonance:

> Blessed art Thou, Lord our God,
> King of the Universe,
> who didst perform miracles for our fathers
> in those days, at this season . . .

On December 17 or 18, Eichmann retreats, leaving Budapest along with his staff; the news reaches Hazalah on the 23rd, but in no way can it be favorably interpreted: the city is almost totally surrounded by the Russians and given over to the Hungarian Nazis, deserters, criminals of all types on the border of insanity—and the fate of the entrapped Jews is more uncertain than ever.

On the 23rd, two Soviet emissaries arrive at a Hungarian military station in the outskirts of Budapest, carrying protective white flags. They bear proposals: the Soviets will spare the city, they will let anyone who so wishes leave for the West, and they will not file suit against the Hungarian military. In exchange, all resistance must cease. The two Russian emissaries—one of them the son of a Hungarian emigrant who went to Russia after the 1919 Bela Kun revolution—are shot down by the Hungarians.

That evening, the siege of Budapest begins. At Hazalah, preparations are made for the final combat. A matter of a few days, they hope. In reality, the nightmare will last more than three weeks. Tens of thousands of Jews will meet death under horrifying conditions, victims of one of the most murderous and most futile battles of the war's end.

TWENTY-FOUR

Desperate Acts

CHRISTMAS ARRIVES, and the war is still not over. The siege of Budapest goes on. Every night a violent shelling and the air attack that follows revive hopes: will liberation come tomorrow? But tomorrow brings the same frozen waiting, and the breath of death. The battle resumes.

Germans and Hungarians, united in this desperate combat, assert that an offensive by General Guderian's armored unit from near Lake Balaton will relieve Budapest. The offensive fails—but it buoys the morale of the besieged. There is also talk of a secret weapon being made ready in Berlin. Thirteen-year-olds are armed. State Secretary Vago declares: "We shall defend Budapest to the end. Every street, every house, every room must become a fortress!"

The defense of the surrounded city fails to divert the Nazis from waging their pitiless war against the Jews: haven't they received the order to exterminate them—to wipe out all witnesses?

A new decree enjoins every Jew living in the Christian city under an assumed identity to appear at one of the ghetto gates. The text includes this note: "Any Hungarian citizen caught in the ghetto without authorization will be executed."

When news of the encirclement of the city is confirmed on Christmas Day the partisans get set for the last battle. For a long time they have known that the attacking force, in closing the pincers, will bring about the start of a final "clean-up" operation. Caught in their own trap, their destiny sealed, the last Nazis will try to drag their enemies down with them to death. And all the Nazi gangs together fall upon the dying ghetto. Death rains from the sky, walks the streets, takes every shape, every face.

At the doors of "protected houses" cluster masses of pleading humans. There are those rescued from the death march, ghetto escapees, Jews whose false identities have been uncovered and have escaped their killers, transfers from other protected houses that have been taken over by the Nazis. There are the old, children, the disabled, the sick. The very bitter cold (on January 1 the thermometer goes down to seven below zero) makes the entreaties even more pathetic.

Messages of distress pile up at Hazalah. Everywhere the Nazis engage in a frantic manhunt. The children's houses are attacked. Most of the occupants are taken to the infamous Raditzsky barracks, the cellars of which have been turned into human slaughterhouses, or to the banks of the Danube. A partisan commando team succeeds in getting some youngsters away from the barracks with the help of fake warrants; the rescued are transported to a hideout on Sziv Street, where until then no raid has taken place. They get there at the end of the day, exhausted and sick. The concierge at the house sees the unfortunates entering; she understands the situation and immediately informs the Nylas. They appear, furious at having been fooled, and kill two children on the spot; the others are lined up, beaten, and dragged to the Danube. This time there is nothing the partisans can do. One of them—an undercover operator among the Nazis—even has to take an active part in the operation; the best he can do is whisper to the strongest of the children, "If you get the chance, escape!"

The chance occurs when the condemned (the oldest is only 15) reach the quay: as prelude to another Russian shelling a flare suddenly lights up the river, which at this point is very wide. The Nylas throw themselves to the ground. With that, 30 or so young ones scatter, following the partisan's advice. The others are shot, and their bodies are swept away by the river as the shelling begins. Three of the escapees, turned in a short time later by another concierge, are taken back to the same place and shot. One of the condemned of the first group, a wounded ten-year-old, manages to save himself by swimming and spending the whole night hanging onto a piling between two blocks of ice.

Death closes in from all sides. Liaison between the various protected houses becomes ever more precarious. The telephones are out of order. Isolated groups sometimes do not know the fate of a nearby group, or even if it is still there.

In the supposed hospital of the Hungarist Legion that Coça Grunwalt keeps in operation on the premises of Cinema City, the situation is difficult; the real Nylas, wounded, flock to the hospital where they mingle with the fake wounded, the fake doctors, the real and fake patients! Otto Fenner, the head doctor (a partisan and a medical student), is overwhelmed with work! But the contact with Nidossy, the Nylas chief of staff, and with his assistant, Nicolas Endre, still functions, and so the Zionists at the hospital know the Nazi password every day (and are quick to pass it on to other Hazalah bases). Nurses—such as Billitzer's sister, Braha—are in charge of the liaison with Vadasz Street, even while the battle rages; the organizers have authentic commissions at their disposal (with Endre's own signature!). In the immense disarray that has seized the city, the existence of a hospital, even an official one, is threatened.

Every day brings its harvest of dramatic news. The list of the captured, the dead, the missing in action grows longer. Of course, no one can keep an accurate count or draw up statistics, but everyone is aware that the hemorrhage has taken on terrible proportions.

At the House of Glass, where all the most daring partisan operations originate, problems of supply are worrisome, the stocks are running low—and just when the refugees are piling in. Elisabeth Eppler decides to stage a raid; a Jew has informed her of the existence of five barrels of butter and several bags of dried peas in an abandoned bunker, about eight miles away. How to get there? She decides to go all out. Several German army trucks are parked in Vadasz Street, where antiaircraft batteries have been installed on the roofs, especially at number 27. Armed with two bottles of Hungarian wine and two hundred Miriam cigarettes, she goes up to the commanding officer. By chance, the officer is young, and an Austrian. Elisabeth introduces herself as an employee of the Swiss legation, offers him her presents, and asks his help in arranging an emergency transport of provisions.

"What about a truck at five o'clock?" the officer says.

"But there are only women at the legation!"

"I'll assign some to help you, miss."

And that is how the barrels and the bags come that very evening to the House of Glass: hauled by German soldiers.

"They carried them all the way up to the attic," Elisabeth says today. "But the most amazing part of the story is that, in this house jammed to bursting with partisans and refugees, the Germans left with the impression that it was empty; they hadn't met a soul!"

Things unfortunately do not always go so well at the House of Glass. Around 10 o'clock, on December 31, a truckload of Nylas stops in front of the garage door, or at least what is left of it (a glass door, it had not withstood the blast of a Russian bomb that had landed nearby). A dozen excited men in green shirts, armed to the teeth, rush shouting into the main courtyard. Of course, this is something for which the partisans are not unprepared, but for all their preparation it is no less frightening. They know from the beginning of the siege that the Nylas have slaughtered all the residents in several protected houses. In the cellars and in the Football Federation bunker next door the partisans lie in wait, close to the few weapons they have in operating order. Arthur Weiss and several leaders try to come to terms with the unit chief, but without success; the Nylas rush down the stairs to the cellar and open fire in the dark. Moans can be heard. Someone barks an order:

"All Jews out! Into the street! Your goose is cooked!"

Has the moment of desperate combat, the one the Zionists have both awaited and feared all these years, finally come, here in the House of Glass? The young partisans decide they should continue to wait.

Slowly the refugees line up along the wall in Vadasz Street. Two or three hundred residents are already outside. The Nylas force the women to give them their handbags and jewels. Arthur Weiss, however, succeeds in engaging the officer in charge in a discussion.

"You don't know what you're doing! You're attacking the Swiss legation!"

Promptly, the Nazis give up their prey. And the arrival of a detachment of Hungarian police, called by Moshe Krausz, saves the Jews lined up in the street; the police chase the Arrow Cross, who withdraw in anger, threatening to return. Returning to the House of Glass, Elisabeth Eppler sees her uncle, a doctor, treating the wounded in the stairway; the mother of Rabbi Schreiber, headmaster of the Budapest rabbinical school, has been badly wounded. Jonas Fenacker was killed instantly. His body will remain in the cellar; the ground is too frozen to bury him. There are other wounded.

This alert has proved that the Nazis know nothing about the Federation bunker. The Zionists can thus continue to use it as a base of operations. But it has also proved the frailty of the protection, now that all law has vanished from Budapest.

And, in fact, the second act takes place the next day. Here is the account of William Weiss, Arthur Weiss's brother:

At the same time, around 10 o'clock, the same truck suddenly appears and forces its way through the gate. It's full of civilians. There is only one soldier among them, a noncom, who asks to speak to Arthur. He demands food: "We know you have supplies, and we, the Nylas, have none." Miraculously, I'm able to get Lutz, the Swiss consul, our protector, on the telephone. I tell him that these civilians seem to me as menacing as the soldiers of the day before. He advises me to call the minister of foreign affairs, but I'm not able to get through. Meanwhile, my brother agrees to turn over two or three bags of food to the Nylas, who lift them into the trucks. The discussion goes on. I understand that the Nazis insist that my brother go with them to Arrow Cross HQ, on Varoshaz Street. I manage to alert Fabry, a Hungarian officer whom we have been paying off in exchange for his protection. He says he will come and, in fact, soon appears at the wheel of a little Topolino. Since the Nylas continue to claim my brother, Fabry advises him to yield. Fabry's last words are, "I give you my word as an officer that Mr. Weiss will return here at 6 P.M." My brother can no longer refuse. He gets into the Topolino. We exchange looks. I think that my brother knew what awaited him; he was sacrificing himself to appease the Nazis and save the House of Glass Resistance. What we heard was that, a short distance from the House of Glass, he was transferred to a truck. Then there was no further trace of him. It's true a violent shelling took place a little after that. No one ever saw my brother Arthur again. And any trace of Fabry too was gone for good.

The last-ditch insurrection spares the House of Glass. But Arthur Weiss has vanished, and the Nylas could return at any moment. Maybe there will not be a second miracle. The partisans stick more and more vigorously to their decision never to give in. The girls are made part of the armed defense network. They undergo military training. For some of them, who will later take part in Israel's war of independence, it is a foretaste of what their lives will be like.

For the Jews, life from now on hangs by a thread; a detail, a coincidence, a mere gesture can be decisive. Two days after Weiss's arrest, a partisan returning from a mission is shot by a patrol at the gate of the House of Glass. It is Alex Furst, who, through tremendous hardship, had succeeded in finding and bringing to the House of Glass a dozen loaves of bread. A few minutes later, the legation's gray "diplomatic car," returning to the base, pulls up to where the poor fellow lies moaning. Three legation employees are in it: Gideon Andor, Tibor Szemere, and Simha Humwald, under the alias of Kühne. Andor goes into the House of Glass, but Humwald and Szemere rush to the aid of their comrade. That is enough to betray them; Nylas, lying in ambush, grab them around their waists and take them away in their own car. Humwald, from Hashomen Hazair, will never return. Those who knew him keep the memory of an indomitable Zionist of unshakable determination. First conscripted into a disciplinary battalion in 1943, he had survived typhus, forced labor, countless harassments, an escape by foot over a distance of more than 600 miles, and innumerable rescue missions. Furst, the messenger, was taken to the House of Glass infirmary and died of his wounds a short while after.

Snow has been falling since the start of the siege. The shellings and air raids succeed one another; planes with the red star (the "Rata") painted on their wings graze the roofs, but the fighting goes on—and so does the massacre. Gangs search for victims. The partisans try to recapture them. Blood flows constantly. On some mornings the Danube is red.

The streets are empty. Budapest resembles a ghost city. Dead bodies are everywhere: victims of the Arrow Cross patrols and also of the strafing from low-flying Russian planes.

Now the Szalasi government itself has left the city. The Hungarian police have almost completely vanished. As for the Arrow Cross, the Nazi looters, the supreme moment arrives, the moment promised by chief Nidossy and so long awaited: total freedom to kill! To kill the Jews.

Starved, sick, dying, the Jews dig into cellars, or into pitiful shelters christened bunkers. In the ghetto nothing moves. The collective kitchens still function—the partisans see to that—but fewer and fewer drag themselves there in the hope of a mess kit filled with hot water and a chunk of cabbage floating in it. Everywhere the city is burning, and the ghetto is in the throes of death. Pest has become a city without life and without soul, a hell of smoking ruins, shattered glass, soiled snow, corpses without graves. A vision of hell.

The liaison between the various protected houses and the bunkers, which is maintained by the partisans, is often cut. Betrayed or discovered, bunkers are raided, defend themselves, and succumb. No prisoners are taken, and no one will ever know the details of these last-ditch fights. (That is how, probably, the Theresa Boulevard bunker disappeared, but the one on Ranolder Street, installed by the partisans in a cellar behind a veritable rampart of barrels, will hold out to the very end with its "garrison" of 20.)

Curfew is at 8 P.M. At night shadows slip in and out among the ruins: partisans on liaison missions, food-supply missions —no one dares to call them rescue missions any longer. From time to time, gunfire signals a skirmish. After the gunfire, silence.

People die of hunger. The animals from the zoo have long

since been consumed; the dead horses are torn to pieces by the famished. There is fighting in Ujpest, in the far suburb. But the siege has gone on for ten days, and so has the battle.

The Hazalah partisans hold out. New groups are formed; they are given the name "strollers." Their game is extremely perilous. Furnished with fake police warrants, they appear in Nylas uniforms at the homes of party dignitaries selected for their cruelty, for their enthusiastic participation in the massacres. Taken by surprise, the Nylas protests his good citizenship, flaunts his service record, brags that he has even pierced Jewish eyes out with red-hot nails. Poker-faced, the strollers reassure him: the "warrant" is surely the result of an error. But they will not be budged. The discussion continues in the street all the way to the first intersection. There the Nazi is executed, though not without having been told the identity of those who kidnapped him. They seize his papers. One more corpse in the snow attracts no attention. Another fake Nazi joins the commandos.

The Russian troops approach. The survivors dig themselves in.

"I couldn't stay still in the cellar though I was relatively safe there," Weiskopf-Horak recalls. "I had food, because many Nazis had asked to be evacuated to the West and had put their supplies up for sale. Every day I went to the ghetto, but it was more and more difficult to get into it. The whole Jewish quarter was said to be mined—the Nylas intended to blow it up with its inhabitants before the arrival of the Russians! I walked like a robot, my teeth clenched. Something forced me to put one foot before the other. I sought out the most famished of the Jews, the most pitiable, and I gave them food. One day, before entering a pillbox where a dozen Jews were struggling against death, I saw Nylas checking the papers of a young boy on the boulevard. I disappeared, keeping close to the walls. My mission accomplished, I came back to the same place. I saw the boy, his dead body hunched up in the snow. His "papers" had failed the test. Another day, I came upon a cart with dozens of corpses piled up in it. The few passersby didn't even turn to look."

Any man who owns a green shirt, a brassard with any kind of insignia on it, a military coat or a revolver can impose his own law. The Zionists exploit this confusion; in the "city park," which the Soviet troops have just reached, furious fighting rages. Germans and Hungarians defend themselves, inch by inch, from tree to tree. Partisans, disguised as "Steel Fist Volunteers," mix with the combatants and, suddenly maneuvering to the rear, enable the Russians to advance. Heroic actions ensue, all the details of which are lost, for they almost always end with the death of the participants.

The order is to take the enemy by surprise, no matter where, no matter how; planned or coordinated operations are out of the question. In the fever of near liberation the partisans throw themselves undisguised—at last—against the enemy! On January 1, Nicolas Deri, alone, attacks with a grenade a detachment of Nazis that has just taken up position. Other partisans literally launch an assault on the Saint-Stephen Boulevard Nylas station. Pinchas Rosenbaum, leading a section of fake Nylas, intervenes on the docks of the Danube, where naked condemned Jews await execution; the partisans claim they have to seize the Jews because, they say, there are Russian spies among them who have to be interrogated. As the real executioners refuse to surrender their prisoners, a fight breaks out—to the benefit of the partisans. A victory! At Hazalah, the word is: for us, every day is the last—before liberation! And each one adds under his breath: or before death!

Nazism lives its last moments in Budapest, but, dying, it still spews forth military and political units, all intent on erecting a barrier against Communism—while, at the same time, fighting among themselves. Small groups, militia, brigades of children, of old men, police units, looting commandos, swarm on all sides. Among these short-lived movements is the Kiska auxiliary unit, whose purpose is to unify all these scattered groups. Under aliases, the partisans gain admission to the Kiskas. They receive equipment of one sort or another and weapons for the last battle. They are assigned to guard duty, at the Red Cross buildings, for instance, and at the very gates of the ghetto! In the evening the partisans, armed, return home, that is, to their Hazalah bases. Of course they also bring precious information, and the passwords.

But soon the Arrow Cross take umbrage at the Kiskas' arrogance. A conflict breaks out. The barracks of the auxiliaries is surrounded. By an amazing coincidence, it is a disguised Hazalah partisan, Ladislas Kepes, who happens to be the guard officer on duty that night. The Nylas officer comes up to him and demands whatever weapons the auxiliary unit has in its possession. Kepes refuses:

"Give you the revolver that was with me on the Russian front? Never! I shot dozens of Jews with it!"

So indignant is his tone, the Nylas chief hesitates, then changes his mind. "Very well. Keep your weapons. But all the officers of the detachment must come with us to headquarters."

And here is the partisan on Arrow Cross premises, at 60 Andrassy Avenue. He is soon face to face with Major Gera, who knows him under another identity, that of Dr. Ladislas Koltai, Hungarian physician in the service of the International Red Cross (for a long time, Kepes has used his first cover for rescue missions). The Nylas dignitary, suspicious and surprised at first, ends by accepting the partisan's story: ashamed of working for the Red Cross in such troubled times, he has committed himself to contribute in a more efficient way to the defense of Budapest and Nazism—and the West. Finally, the major congratulates the partisan. Danger is averted, though not for good. The Arrow Cross has decided to dissolve the Kiska unit, into which they suspect the Jews, taking advantage of the disarray of the police services, have infiltrated. Jews! Kepes is indignant: he has seen them at the Red Cross. They are usually cowards who run and hide at the first sound of gunfire! You must have heard the saying, "Make a move with your hand, and the Jew will move with his feet."

Major Gera then utters words that Kepes, his expression still contemptuous, hears with pride:

"You're right, Doctor. But I hear there are Zionists who are different—even brave, they say."

Kepes shrugs his shoulders.

The conflict with the Arrow Cross is rapidly settled; the Kiskas, with a Nylas cadre, are ordered to take part in missions to defend the city park, where Soviet vanguards are applying heavy pressure. Major Gera insists that the sector be placed under the command of the former doctor, now an exemplary officer—Kepes! The partisan leaves at the head of his auxiliaries; he posts his guard in especially open and untenable positions—and deserts at the end of the afternoon. He joins his group's base on Benczur Street. That very night, disguised as a Gestapo special agent, he leaves with five Hazalah comrades upon a new rescue operation: two tortured prisoners await death in the cellars of the secret police on City Hall Street.

TWENTY-FIVE

The Last Fighting

ON JANUARY 13, a Russian patrol reaches the building at 16 Benczur Street, quarters of the "Red Cross Transport Section," one of the Hazalah bases, and office of the "Swedish Legation for Hungary Liberated by the Red Army." Raoul Wallenberg, for weeks the most efficient support the partisans have, is in the building; he asks to be put in touch with the Soviet command. He will disappear some time afterward and will never be heard of again.

At Hazalah, in the new situation, total priority is given to the food missions; behind its fence, the ghetto is dying. They know that Russian soldiers have penetrated the eastern suburbs of Pest and are advancing through the underground, the cellars, and the sewers toward the ghetto. But intense fighting delays their arrival.

During the nights of January 17th and 18th, elements of the Red Army under an intense artillery barrage from the Germans, who have retreated to the hilltops of Buda, at last reach the fence along Wesselenyi Street. They discover the Jewish quarter, silent, as though paralyzed, an agonizing stench of death arising from it.

It is indeed the end—but it comes too late. The curtain falls on too much suffering, too much despair, too many innocent deaths, too many corpses without graves.

The partisans, who also enter the ghetto, remain watchful; the Nazi uniform that saved their lives yesterday now becomes a target for Russian bullets. Firing comes from all sides; the rattling of Tommy guns crackles uninterruptedly. Sometimes the partisans see an Arrow Cross detachment retreating before Russian scouts, taking with them Jews whom they use as living shields; the Russians, indifferent, fire and shoot down the whole group, women and children alike. The dead of the last days are beyond counting. And so are the living; paralyzed, frozen, half-conscious, they blend with the rubble in the ghetto.

It is the end of a nightmare, but will the nightmare stop? With great care, the partisans make a check of the hideouts, the bunkers, the fortified cellars. They often find dead bodies there. In one basement are four young Jewish girls, raped, their bellies split open. The Nazis committed suicide on the site of their apocalyptic bacchanal. The ritual baths, where pious Jews gathered to utter their praises of God, have become a kind of morgue for frozen corpses. Death is ever present. Only the severe cold keeps a frightful epidemic from breaking out. The partisans call the role of the living. But they themselves must show the greatest prudence: how could the Russians know with whom they are dealing? Through a strange reversal of the situation, the Nylas and the Hungarian Nazis now disguise themselves as Jews, sporting the Star of David, in order to escape their fate.

The Nazi combatants fall back on Buda, but before leaving they still make efforts to kill. One execution follows another in the basement of City Hall, on Varoshaz Street, in the barracks, in the Nylas stations, in Margrit prison. The young surviving Jews scatter throughout the city. Some even manage to make themselves look like Russians, with a fur cap and a red star. The presses issue new documents—Russian this time—certificates, safe-conducts, intended to grant the bearers the protection of the occupying police.

There is no way to use cars, even diplomatic cars. The last Germans in Pest, the Hungarians, the Russians, shoot any vehicle on sight. The partisans go out by foot, at random, into the raging battle. Nobody speaks anymore of planning, of retreat, of a "cover," no matter how tenuous. It is an all-out hunt for life in the dying, famished, frozen city, where the manhunt prevails. Many partisans will lose their lives in this last-ditch action: in the cellars of City Hall street, for instance, where the "liberators" who have smashed through the defenses are shot down, along with those they had come to rescue.

On the 18th, the liberation of Pest is complete. Russian soldiers tear down the Kiraly Street fence. Nicolas Birnbaum, a partisan, is there; he mixes with the Russian soldiers. One of them addresses him in Yiddish:

"I'm a Ukrainian," the soldier says. "My father was *hazan* [a cantor in the synagogue] . . . it's been a long time since I spoke Yiddish."

Later, in a hideout where the Jews hesitate to believe in the end of their ordeal, the soldier will sing for them the canticle of the dead, *El Mole Rashamin* ("God is full of mercy!").

The Russians are now masters of the city and the ghetto. The survivors do not easily emerge from their cellars, hideouts, shelters. They open their eyes to a landscape of disaster.

Ukrainian soldiers tear down the last planks. Can one believe in peace? From Buda, the shelling goes on. The Russians respond with mortar fire. Tanks rumble through the wreckage.

The Danube cannot be crossed. Bits of information reach the Hazalahs, however. The Nylas terror rages now in Buda. When discovered, Jews are attacked, tortured, executed. In their retreat the Nazis liquidate the remaining hospitals and sanatoria. Gangs of killers, retreating from Pest, carry out blind massacres. Doctors, nurses, children, the sick are shot down in the wards. Horrifying scenes unfold. The able-bodied Jews are forced to dig trenches and stuff corpses into them. The Nazis then line them up and shoot them.

Buda will not be occupied by the Russians until February 13. The voices of the cannons fade away, and the silence brooding over the city is disturbed only by a few detonations. The capital of Hungary—what remains of it—is free. It is victory. Peace. But in the protected houses, in the Hazalah bases, in the few bunkers that have held out, there are no bursts of joy. Just the opposite, in fact: an immense sadness. For the Zionists who survived this unequal fight, liberation and victory have the taste of ashes. True, lives have been saved; the Nazi plan of extermination has been cut short; nearly 69,000 Jews are alive in the ghetto. In Budapest, a total of 125,000 Jews have escaped physical liquidation. But how many died? And how many Hazalah partisans have perished in combat?

For the living, moreover, some risk remains. In the ghetto, the famine is terrible. People die of hunger in the streets. One sees veritable skeletons walking around, where only the eyes give any sign of life. Many liberated Jews are ill. Many have lost the desire to live.

Hazalah has attained its objectives, at the cost of immense sacrifices. Malinovski's and Tolboukhine's soldiers occupy the ruins of Budapest. The hour of the so-long-awaited liberation strikes.

But the Soviet liberators raise new problems. The conquest of Budapest has cost them 30,000 dead. Accustomed to shooting, they sometimes shoot at shadows. Having killed so many times to defend their lives, they now kill for nothing: a leather coat, boots, a watch, a bottle of liquor. A suspicious gesture, a false maneuver triggers their fire. Budapest is a jungle of stone, where the strongest imposes the law. Every civilian raises suspicion; the partisans who bring food to the sick and the dying in the ghetto run other risks. Life, justice, happiness, have not reasserted themselves. In the eyes of the world the Jews of Budapest have been liberated. Hazalah saved many of them. But are they safe?

The sun in those first days of February pierces the clouds. But for the surviving partisans who turn their eyes to the future, toward Israel, and for the others, nothing has ended. The Jews have learned to attach more importance to threats than to promises. They have paid with millions of dead for one of the most tragic lessons in the history of mankind. The extermination in Europe, and especially in Hungary, will not be merely a memory. A dream will become reality: Zionism. To the last moanings along the banks of the Danube, along the Budapest-Vienna road, to the last of those asphyxiated at Auschwitz, the announcement of the creation of the Jewish State will soon answer like an echo. The vast majority of the Hungarian Zionists, Hazalah survivors, will meet again in Israel. Many will die there during the war of independence. Others will settle in the kibbutzim. Some will rise to important positions. Today they are about 40 or 50 years old, and they have to be coaxed to recount their memories. One of these survivors, however, learning that this book was being written, insisted on giving me a notebook in Yiddish. It was in Jerusalem. The man, tired, had come from a kibbutz on the border.

"These are the notes of my brother," he said. "He was young, and a Hazalah partisan, in Budapest. One day, he failed to return from a rescue mission. I am the sole survivor of our family, and this notebook is all that I brought with me. After I'm gone, it won't interest anyone anymore."

The day before his last mission, the boy—brother of all those who worked for Hazalah—wrote that he'd be 20 years old in six months, and that he hoped to celebrate his birthday in Israel, with a girl, in the sun.

Selected Bibliography

Studies of the Yad Washem Institute, Jerusalem.
Records from the trials of Szalasi, Veesenmeyer, Krumay, and Eichmann.
Archives of the Ministry of Foreign Affairs, Third Reich.
General Encyclopedia (in Yiddish).

Biss, A. *Un Million de Juifs à sauver* (Grasset).
Derogy, J. *La Loi du Retour* (Fayard).
Levai, E. *Destin Juif en Hongrie* (L. P. Davis).
———. *Livre Noir* (L. P. Davis).
Morse, A. *Pendant que six millions mouraient* (Laffont).
Poliakoff, L. *Bréviaire de la Haine* (Calmann-Levy).
Ringelblum, E. *Chronique du Ghetto de Varsovie* (Laffont).
Sabille, J. *Lueurs dans la Tourmente* (Edition du Centre).
Skorzeny, O. *Missions secrètes* (Flammarion).
Steinberg, L. *La Révolte des Justes* (Fayard).
Weissberg, Alex. *Historie de Joel Brandt* (Seuil).
Wormser-Migot, O. *Le Système concentrationnaire nazi* (P.U.F.).

Index